ANCIENT GODDESS MAGIC

"This beautiful book is a remembering of the goddess who is not only an earth mother but also a cosmic mother. It's a reminder that so many of our ancestral feminine traditions were focused on astro-oracles, women who looked to the stars for guidance and divination and who were mistresses of reading the patterns of the interweaving living planetary intelligences."

SEREN BERTRAND, AUTHOR OF *SPIRIT WEAVER*
AND COAUTHOR OF *WOMB AWAKENING*

ANCIENT GODDESS MAGIC

)O(

INVOKING THE QUEENS OF THE HEAVENS

A Sacred Planet Book

VANESSA LAVALLÉE

Destiny Books
Rochester, Vermont

Destiny Books
One Park Street
Rochester, Vermont 05767
www.DestinyBooks.com

Text stock is SFI certified

Destiny Books is a division of Inner Traditions International

Sacred Planet Books are curated by Richard Grossinger, Inner Traditions editorial board member and cofounder and former publisher of North Atlantic Books. The Sacred Planet collection, published under the umbrella of the Inner Traditions family of imprints, includes works on the themes of consciousness, cosmology, alternative medicine, dreams, climate, permaculture, alchemy, shamanic studies, oracles, astrology, crystals, hyperobjects, locutions, and subtle bodies.

Cataloging-in-Publication Data for this title is available from the Library of Congress

ISBN 978-1-64411-645-6 (print)
ISBN 978-1-64411-646-3 (ebook)

Printed and bound in the United States by Lake Book Manufacturing, LLC
The text stock is SFI certified. The Sustainable Forestry Initiative® program promotes sustainable forest management.

10 9 8 7 6 5 4 3 2 1

Text design and layout by Priscilla Harris Baker
This book was typeset in Garamond Premier Pro with Cinzel, Futura, Gill Sans, and Legacy Sans used as display typefaces

Potnia Theron amphora photo (page 50) and Nebra sky disc photo (page 138) courtesy of Wikimedia Commons (CC BY-SA 4.0)

To send correspondence to the author of this book, mail a first-class letter to the author c/o Inner Traditions • Bear & Company, One Park Street, Rochester, VT 05767, and we will forward the communication, or contact the author directly at **VanessaLavallee.com/contact**.

Scan the QR code and save 25% at InnerTraditions.com. Browse over 2,000 titles on spirituality, the occult, ancient mysteries, new science, holistic health, and natural medicine.

I started writing this book after returning from Greece in 2021. Inspiration came from the stars and the sea and the magical island of Aegina. Three years later, my deepest gratitude goes to my husband and my baby daughter who showed tremendous patience while I was working on this book through the numerous Covid waves we endured. I would also like to thank my colleagues and professors who inspired me and my students who are able to keep up with my never-ending ideas and never-ending anxieties. Finally, I am thankful to the Inner Traditions team who showed great patience and professionalism with me in this first publishing experience.

CONTENTS

MY PATH TO THE ANCIENT GODDESS MYSTERIES

The idea for this book was born out of two different passions of mine. The first, based on my graduate work about ancient Mediterranean demons and goddesses, was my desire to reconsider and explore in a new light the many ancient goddesses of the Mediterranean. Some of them are quite popular today among goddess spirituality movements and practitioners of contemporary witchcraft, but others have been forgotten. I wanted to get rid of traditional interpretations and demonstrate that the divine feminine in the ancient world was not solely based on fertility roles—quite the contrary, in fact. When I was studying ancient religions at the University of Wales, the wonderful professors there introduced me to the fascinating world of archaeoastronomy. This unique program at the Sophia Centre led by excellent archaeologists and historians is focused on the ancient cultural history of the sky. It was in Wales, where many ancient sites are in tune with the sky, that I realized that many myths of ancient deities were connected to the stories of constellations and celestial objects and that our modern interpretation of these ancient cultural stories had partially forgotten this connection.

My second passion is in astral magic and how to use the sky as a powerful healing tool. My interest in astronomy and myth goes back to 1996, when I began practicing astrology. My interest in astrology in part prompted my research into ancient ritual texts from Mesopotamian, Hittite, Greek, and even Northern European cultures. Eventually, I noticed how their worldview and practices were often focused on celestial objects and that they understood the influence those astral powers have over us. Although this field needs more investigation, over the years I have sought to rediscover this ancient knowledge and to share and practice some forms of astral magic.

How can we connect ancient goddess history and astral magic? Ancient goddesses have always been an inspiration to me, especially the warrior goddesses. I felt drawn to this original feminine energy that was assertive and sometimes aggressive and represented a powerful combative force within women that scared most men. Very early in life, I started to communicate with the nonhuman world—mostly trees, the wind and stars, and, of course, animals—but I didn't think anything of it. It was a natural way of being in the world for me. Years later I had a dream that inspired me and led me to believe that energies can manifest through us. In the dream, a loud feminine voice clearly told me to teach her story, and then the dream ended. This message surprised me as I was just starting my studies and did not have, at the time, any specific interest in goddesses other than a profound respect. Like many people, for a long time I believed the narrative about the power of the feminine being limited to fertility. I then decided to study ancient goddesses during my undergraduate work to help me understand why I would need to teach something different about the feminine. I finally understood, while pursuing religious studies and then archaeology of ancient religions, that there was something off in our conventional interpretations of powerful ancient goddesses.

Since 2014 I have dedicated my time to studying ancient goddesses and the materiality of magic. I am currently working on a thesis about the demonic feminine and hold several conferences a year on the subject of ancient magic and the story of the feminine. My research has led me to observe that these ancient goddesses were very often connected to patterns and symbols that were associated with specific stars and constellations. Of course, this book is not exhaustive: Each goddess could have been an entire book, and there are many more goddesses associated with powerful celestial objects and constellations beyond the ones I cover here. Understanding these goddesses is a lifetime of work, and I think we will never completely understand them.

In this book, I provide a brief overview of important goddesses and how their symbolism connects with myths and celestial patterns. Although I present some historical references, the interpretation of the symbolic patterns is personal and spiritual. The celestial patterns have different significance in other cultures and bear other names. The southern sky also has different stories; this work is focused primarily on a specific part of the world that greatly influenced the cultural development of Europe and Western Asia. The function of the stars remains the same around the world, but the interpretation will vary greatly. My approach stems from the religious studies field, in which patterns and symbolism are compared.

I have divided the celestial goddesses into four major categories or symbolic patterns—the creatrix, the warrior, the healer, and the lady of the sea—along with their connections to the divine solar and lunar feminine aspects. I have chosen those goddesses and their respective celestial bodies according to the type of magic and power they hold. You will notice that they all have in common the ability to connect with the underworld and the dead, to protect the deceased and assist with spiritual rebirth and regeneration. I have tried to incorporate what seemed to me to be good preparation to understand death by connecting with those forces that guide us through the last portal. At the end of each chapter, I have outlined what symbolic message and way of connecting correspond to each goddess pattern.

As you will see, each goddess carries many aspects and has different roles. Nevertheless, the applied symbolic categories serve the purpose of representing how these celestial energies were used for different types of magic. Goddesses were the manifestations of the power of those constellations and therefore had cults dedicated to them based on those stellar objects and other natural elements. It is important to note that this type of magic is by no means a replacement to seek medical advice for any physical or mental illnesses. The ancient healers used these types of rituals and medicine to help with physical ailments, but it was mostly a spiritual healing that was leading them to better health. We cannot attest that it was efficient, but ancient medicine is also a field that needs more research.

Another important note is that the ancients really believed that the celestial bodies were their gods and thought of themselves as servants to them. The deities associated with planets were not meant to be symbolic: the planets were true deities holding powers and influences. This applied as well to other types of spirits because the European worldviews before the seventeenth century were mostly animist, although magic was practiced in a Christian culture—this is what we call "folk magic." I use the term *animism* in the new anthropological definition. Animism was how we used to comprehend the world, and to some extent, some people continue to relate to the world this way. This view was based on a relationship with nature as our ancestors understood we were one with it. It was not to ascribe a human soul to nature but to sense and feel the energy that emanates from the living world.

Finally, in the chapter "Celestial Healing" are examples of rituals for celestial invocation and bathing and for connecting with the underworld. The rituals and spells were inspired by ancient Mesopotamian, Egyptian, Hittite, and Greek texts, which I have adapted for modern use. The objects that I suggest making, such as amulets and statues, are inspired from archaeological finds. I have adapted these rituals and objects because we relate to the divine differently today. We no longer sacrifice animals, for example, and we no longer need to destroy cities (although it still happens).

I hope you enjoy this book and see it as a spiritual tool to enhance your knowledge and worship of some ancestral goddesses and their energies. My only goal with this book is to inspire us to think about other ways of understanding the divine feminine.

Les étoiles du matin, by Sarah Paxton Ball Dodson, 1887

MEETING THE QUEENS OF THE HEAVENS

No one knows what has existed and has vanished beyond recovery, evidence for the number of times Man has understood and has forgotten again that his mind and flesh and life and movements are made of star stuff, sun stuff, planet stuff.

DORIS LESSING,
BRIEFING FOR A DESCENT INTO HELL, 1971

Imagine that you are walking barefoot in the sand. You can feel the waves touching your feet. You hear the ships entering the harbor, and familiar scents of herbs and spices are wafting from the market. When you look ahead, you see the temple of the tutelary goddess of your city. You feel the heat of the sun touching your skin, and you sense the immense power this great radiant ball of fire has. You see the sun disappear behind the sea, and then you wonder what land lies beneath the water. You know that she, the sun, will bring all of today's deceased souls into this land of no return. As Venus, the herald of the night, announces the coming of the moon, you lift your eyes toward the sky, and there they are—the stars. The goddesses are watching you.

Queen of Heaven was a title in the ancient world. More specifically, it was a title that many goddesses shared, especially if they were related to the sky. Such a strong title can only make us wonder how powerful and important some ancient goddesses were for their worshippers. The Christian Virgin Mary inherited this title, a reminder of the powerful pre-Christian queens of the heavens.

In the current era, during which patriarchal dominance has prevailed, it can be challenging to envision a time when women held significant power. However, in the past century, there has been a growing interest in ancient goddesses thanks in part to advances in scholarship. While in antiquity there was no singular great goddess cult, the presence and importance of goddesses in the ancient world cannot be denied. All those goddesses were autonomous, but they still existed in a pantheon full of male gods as well. It is important to understand that balance was achieved by determined roles for each divinity and its nature. This book explores the inherent powers of some of these goddesses, which were deeply intertwined with nature and the cosmos.

In our modern understanding, the divine is often perceived as a transcendent and distant entity, typically depicted as an anthropomorphic male deity. This is the prevailing perception for most individuals. We tend to envision spirits as entities that exist beyond a veil. However, it is important to note that the concept of a distant spiritual realm emerged during the Victorian era, when it was deemed such knowledge needed to be concealed in an invisible otherworldly kingdom.

Our ancestors perceived spirits and deities as real sentient beings from nature. The veil between the worlds was not an abstract concept; it was a physical manifestation, seen as the mist descending from the highest mountain or slowly moving over a lake. The world of ancient peoples was full of simultaneous dangers and blessings. The sky was of particular importance, something we moderns have completely forgotten. Indeed, researchers tend to overlook the importance that the night sky had in ancient times because we mostly can't see it anymore. The constellations and stars that were revered by our ancestors continue to exist, but we don't learn about them as much as we did before, and we certainly do not know where they are in the firmament. This simple fact is the reason why we tend to analyze the ancient world through a lens that has forgotten that deities were once very present and real for our ancestors.

During the emergence of early civilizations, the practice of writing and using seals as a means of communication with other kingdoms was already established. It is noteworthy that constellations were already known by specific names, passed down through age-old wisdom. The exact origins of this astronomical knowledge being transmitted through oral history cannot be precisely traced. According to the UNESCO world heritage sites program, some clusters of stars were recognized quite early on. During the Upper Paleolithic era, certain star patterns like Corona Borealis, the Pleiades, and the Hyades were not only identified but also played a significant role in timekeeping and navigation. One well-known example of possible depictions of the Pleiades and Hyades can be found in the aurochs painting in the Hall of the Bulls at Lascaux cave in France.

Another important find was a very old lunar calendar, possibly dating from 35,000 BCE, indicating to scientists that the moon was used to mark time very early on. This discovery led archaeologists to reflect on the profound connection between the mathematical realm and the realm of the gods, as it pertains to human existence.

Since the Upper Paleolithic era, and possibly even earlier, humans have bestowed profound symbolic and mythical significance upon the celestial expanse enveloping our planet. The connection between revered animals and their representation in the celestial realms has long been recognized. Initially depicted in cave paintings, we now have knowledge of one of the oldest temples in existence, Göbekli Tepe, which served as an astronomical sanctuary. Within this temple, colossal pillars bear intricate carvings of various animal figures. This indicates that the constellations resembling animals were regarded as sacred and held great importance, preceding their later depiction in human form. Standing beneath the starry night sky, this temple, dating back twelve thousand years, is a tangible testament to the profound influence and reverence ancient humans attributed to the celestial bodies. Göbekli Tepe was indeed used to commemorate the ascent of the radiant Sirius at midsummer, a celestial event of great significance at the time, since it was a new star born in the sky (Magli 2016). One can only wonder about those ancient rituals held under the night sky.

There is another structure, dating from about 7500 BCE, that was discovered in Egypt in Nabta Playa. This megalithic site is believed to follow the solstice, leading the sun through burial chambers. The stone circle was once also aligned to Arcturus, Sirius, and Alpha Centauri. On this site are found circled stones that seemed to correspond to the constellation Orion (Malville 1998). A cult dedicated to Hathor may have taken place there during the rise of the Egyptian kingdom, and she was revered in her form as the Milky Way, seen by the Egyptians as a celestial cow. Already by the fifth millennium BCE, it seems that the northern sky was of great importance to nomadic tribes, and the Egyptians came to believe that the Milky Way was the land of immortality: "Interest in the northern part of the heavens does indeed seem pervasive during the Late and Terminal Neolithic at Nabta Playa and Gebel Ramlah. The northern circumpolar region of the sky is that realm where stars never set, and, later in dynastic Egypt, it became identified as the realm of eternal life" (Malville 2007, 7).

In a study of African beliefs from the Cape Town region in South Africa, inhabitants exemplified how the stars were important in their culture, as cited here:

> Celestial bodies developed from a mythological past in which stars, planets, people and animals had a common origin. Explanations of the movements of stellar bodies (e.g. sun, moon and Milky Way) are based on keen observations which are simultaneously anthropomorphic and anthropocentric in character. Stars and other entities have will and intention, even speech, and their 'behaviour' is perceived as responsive to human needs and intervention, hence the necessity for people to interact with the moon and certain stars to secure food. Certain celestial bodies are filled with supernatural potency that influence people's good fortune in everyday life. (Hollman 2007, 11)

This reflects very well how I imagine people from the past interacting with celestial bodies.

This was the beginning of a widespread cult relating to the sun and stars. We will explore that in the forthcoming chapters. In the following centuries, the ancient megalithic cultures developed at the same rate, and more than thirty-five thousand sites like this, in Europe alone, were found all along the Atlantic and Mediterranean coasts, the most popular one being Stonehenge in England, another site famous for its alignment with solstices.

The main feature of all these sites is that they are very often located near burial chambers. These ancient sites have been sacred locations for ritual purposes—possibly funerary ones because archaeologists have found numerous offerings and tombs on site (Sánchez-Quinto et al. 2019). Many of these megalithic structures have an important relation to the sun, as the solstices are a time where the sun passes through the chambers or doorways. The fact that tombs and stone circles followed the direction of the sun indicates a strong connection to the sky. Evidence from tombs suggests that kings and fallen warriors received post-mortem honorific cults, such as ancestor cults, on site. Celestial bathing and healing were also possibly practiced there.

FINDING ANCIENT GODDESSES IN MODERN TIMES

Ancient tombs and cult sites often contain a significant number of goddess, or feminine, figurines. This abundance led archaeologists in the twentieth century to consider the possibility of a widespread mother goddess religion in prehistoric times. The Neolithic period marked a crucial shift in ancient cultures and religious beliefs. It was during this period that we find substantial evidence of goddess-related religions, with a particular emphasis on death and rebirth rituals, which would influence subsequent millennia.

Arthur Evans, an archaeologist, popularized the notion of a prevalent great goddess cult in the Minoan culture of Crete. While his findings have been criticized for inaccuracies, his interpretation was somewhat intuitive as he discovered numerous objects depicting a female deity that appeared to hold a prominent position. Notable examples include the well-known Minoan snake goddess and the depiction of a mountain goddess on gold coins. Marija Gimbutas, an archaeologist from Lithuania, studied the European Neolithic cultures and also came to the conclusion that the ancient world seemed to have revered female figures. She interpreted the many artifacts she studied as different aspects of one great goddess. She was right about the patterns, though ancient goddesses had many forms and functions. Both Evan and Gimbutas were not correct about a "Great Goddess" religion. Gimbutas has been criticized for her turn to the great goddess theories, but it was in the air by the time she was a professor. Second-wave feminism in the United States prompted this theory. Many scholars have since proven that the hypothesis of a great goddess is not valid, but it remains popular, especially in modern paganism.

In the early twentieth century, when archaeology was booming, the many finds of ancient nude female statuettes in the Mediterranean led researchers to interpret these figurines as representing fertility goddesses and proof that a nature and fertility cult was common in the ancient world (Stavrakopoulou 2017). In the 1970s with the rise of feminism, the idea that the world was once dominated by a great goddess religion became very popular, and it suddenly made sense for many women to turn to a new spirituality as an alternative to mainstream religions. This led to a spiritual "goddess movement," which has continued to grow ever since. People from many different backgrounds are now following a spiritual path linked to goddesses and very often see Earth (Gaia) as an embodiment of her. Many modern interpretations of the goddess in academia, but mostly outside it, are still based on the idea that she is a symbol of fertility and motherhood.

Historically, the idea that all goddesses are the same aspect of one goddess started only during late antiquity with the rise of Isis. Before that, the ancients knew and revered different goddesses and all of their aspects, which is why we find thousands of different goddesses in the early Bronze Age. Deities were found in sacred groves and near springs and trees. Over time, more popular goddesses absorbed the functions of other less well-known goddesses, a process called syncretism. Because of this process, fewer and fewer goddesses survived over time (Asher-Greve 2013). This led to the idea of a singular goddess with many aspects. Isis, for example, became that figure, the almighty one who, by the end of late antiquity, had absorbed all of the other deities' powers. We can see this interpretation of Isis as representing every goddess of the ancient world in the novel *Metamorphoses* by Lucius Apuleius (bk. 11, chap. 47), dating from the second century CE:

> I am she that is the natural mother of all things, mistress and governess of all the elements, the initial progeny of worlds, chief of powers divine, Queen of Heaven, the principal of the Gods celestial, the light of the goddesses: at my will the planets of the air, the wholesome winds of the Seas, and the silences of hell be disposed; my name, my divinity is adored throughout all the world in divers manners, in variable customs and in many names, for the Phrygians call me Pessinuntica, the mother of the Gods: the Athenians call me Cecropian Artemis: the Cyprians, Paphian Aphrodite: the Candians, Dictyanna: the Sicilians, Stygian Proserpine: and the Eleusians call me Mother of the Corn. Some call me Juno, others Bellona of the Battles, and still others Hecate. Principally the Ethiopians which dwell in the Orient, and the Egyptians which are excellent in all kinds of ancient doctrine, and by their proper ceremonies accustomed to worship me, do call me Queen Isis. Behold I am come to take pity of thy fortune and tribulation, behold I am present to favor and aid thee. Leave off thy weeping and lamentation, put away thy sorrow, for behold the healthful day, which is ordained by my providence, therefore be ready to attend to my commandment.*

We can understand in this powerful statement from the goddess Isis that she became the embodiment of all heavens, seas, and the underworld goddesses. Since then, the idea that the different divinities are manifestations of a single deity has stayed in the cultural mind and was revived by the end of the eighteenth century.

Since the revival of ancient paganism, which started in the early modern

---

*This is an adaption by Paul Halsall of a translation by the sixteenth-century scholar William Adlington.

period, all goddesses have been reenvisioned and transformed into versions of a great goddess of nature. The fact that archaeologists from the nineteenth and twentieth centuries assumed that all goddesses found in the Mediterranean and Europe were fertility deities made this narrative very persistent. Where white Christian men saw nudity and femininity, they understood sexual depravity and fertile mothers (Stavrakopoulou 2017). Every goddess was seen as an aspect of the great Mesopotamian mother goddess, which spread all around the Mediterranean. Although there is some truth in this—goddesses did move to other lands, especially from the East to the West—this assumption has greatly reduced our understanding of the influence and importance that ancient goddesses would have had in ancient times. This reductive vision is still applied to modern women today, as if fertility and motherhood were the only things of importance to women. That is quite ironic because ancient fertility figures were mostly males.

The seeds or sperm cells in male semen were understood as creators of life, and therefore a lot of male fertility figures were also associated with nature (Budin 2015). Indeed, the male principle was more often associated with the spirits of farmland and forests and Earth itself. This can be seen in Neolithic times, with the procreative force manifesting in male demons and spirits of all genres, horned deities, and fauns. Gods such as Baal and El, rain and storm gods, were symbolic representations of the fertile powers of the rain. Most Goddesses, meanwhile, were, for quite some time, more often associated with the heavenly skies, especially the night sky—before the male sky gods overturned their sovereignty. The ancient Egyptians viewed the ground as male and the sky as female, a common ancient conception of the world before it somehow got switched around in other cultures. Now the female is seen as more passive and is linked with Earth while god the father is in the sky. This notion is deeply ingrained even in the feminist spirituality of today's world: the Earth has become the ultimate goddess.

This book is an attempt to overcome this problem. First, I aim to encourage the idea that the ancient world was animist, and today's world should continue to be. We can see that the animist worldview managed to survive the Middle Ages and continues to exist today in some cultures and practices. Second, I would like to demonstrate that the divine feminine does not dwell only in the passive form of mothers and maiden lovers, just being present to receive the male energy, with the focus on the womb only. This is a very modern narrative of the sacred feminine. Brilliant scholar Ronald Hutton demonstrated in his recent work, *Queens of the Wild*, that the Mother Earth archetype was an invention of the pagan revival of nineteenth-century scholarship.* Even though the mostly Athenian and Delphic Gaia appeared in Greece by the fifth century BCE, she did not have cults as a universal "Mother Earth goddess equivalent" (Draper 2020). To better understand the switch in the narrative, I take a more philosophical approach in this book, exploring the different ways to conceive and relate to the cosmos and the divine feminine and, mostly, how we can appease our fears about the passage of time and the imminence of death.

As such, the human mind is a fascinating tool that has used the same symbolic patterns to make sense of the world since the beginning of humanity. In the anthropological study of the imaginary, anthropologist Gilbert Durand deciphered how humans repeat and understand images and symbols the same way in every culture and generation of humans. This theory demonstrates very well that the human mind sees the world as an eternal duality between a nocturnal regime and a diurnal one. This dual scheme is then developed into three aspects that are of great importance to humans: digestion, sexuality, and death. Images produced by the human mind are therefore different but always represent at the core the same symbolic meaning. These symbols and images are both inspired by the bodily senses of humans and by the environment surrounding them. In an animistic worldview, these imagery and symbolic markers will therefore be very similar in every culture. This, in part, explains why we will find so many divinities and spirits that carry the same functions and symbolic meanings. As you will notice, many goddesses share similar characteristics even though they are from different cultures. As for their link with constellations and stars, we will observe how the feminine is very often related to the night sky; hence why celestial objects of the night are of importance to

---

*If you would also like to learn more about how contemporary paganism and witchcraft still plays the fertility goddess narrative that was invented in the nineteenth and twentieth-century scholarship, Ronald Hutton's *Triumph of the Moon* is also a must.

understand them. As such, women worshipped all these night goddesses and performed rituals during the nighttime. Water, birds of prey, caverns, and holes are also feminine elements shared with darkness.

This book will shed light on some of the most well-known ancient goddesses but also on some who are forgotten today. My previous research highlighted that most female deities of the ancient world held great magical and political powers although they existed in a male-dominated pantheon. It is quite important to know and understand because procreation was not always a focus in ancient times, especially in Mesopotamia where they thought the cities were already overpopulated. Of course, there are motherhood figures, protecting pregnant women and their children, but they themselves were very often not literal mothers. They may have sometimes helped to bring fertility to humans or to the agricultural lands through intermediate relations with the male gods (Budin 2015).

To understand ancient deities, it is also valuable to understand how ancient religions worked. Mesopotamia is always a good starting point because it had the greatest influence on many religions of the ancient world. As a matter of fact, ancient Greeks and Romans, among them Pliny the Elder, told us that magic came from the East and spread to the Western world. The same happened to a lot of the Eastern deities who entered the Greek pantheon later. It is mostly because of the commercial trade routes that sailors, like the Phoenicians for example, spread knowledge of magic and religious cults throughout Europe.*

A MULTICULTURAL AND ANIMISTIC WORLD

The history of the ancient world is complex, and the purpose of this work is not to explore every detail of this rich and long history—although I would like to. Suffice it to say that there are discernible patterns that can help us gain better insights. For example, in the literature of Sumer, one of the earliest civilizations, we have found lists of thousands of goddesses. What we can gather from this literature is that Sumerian culture was

---

*For further reading on this subject, see Aruz, Graff, and Rakic, *Cultures in Contact: From Mesopotamia to the Mediterranean in the Second Millennium B.C.*

profoundly nature based and animistic, and the Sumerians believed they needed to maintain the cosmos through service to the gods. Humans were thought to have been crafted from a mix of clay and blood through the ingenuity of the goddess of life and the god of wisdom. In these early texts, written in Sumerian, one of the oldest languages, we can find stories about how the night sky was of great importance in healing and how planets, stars, constellations, and the twilight and dawn were all thought to be deities. Reflecting the importance of the heavenly writings of the night sky, archaic texts from Sumeria tell us about a very ancient goddess named Nisaba. She was the scribe of heaven and interested in the interpretation of the stars (Asher-Greve 2013, 43).

The information I have gathered since 2014, when I began studying the ancient world, indicates to me that the evolution of goddess worship in the various Bronze Age cultures was remarkably similar. The first goddesses were almost always venerated individually at first. When the Akkadian people took over the ancient Sumerian land to form the first great empire, the goddesses were gradually given male consorts. However, the relationships between these goddesses and their god-like consorts cannot be interpreted like human relationships: these consorts were not literal lovers or siblings but rather represented another side of the same deity. A brother and sister divine duo were almost always the same deity, each representing a different role and aspect. Various myths about these divine duos involve incest, but in fact, the incest was not understood as literal. The ancient world had a complex literature with more genres than we have today, making it difficult for us to understand the meaning of their narratives. That is why it can take a lifetime for scholars to correctly understand just one text.

In the study of ancient religions, it is always better to look at all the data and not just the texts. We sometimes forget that writing was very often politically motivated, intended to impose an idea or worldview on the population. It was used as political propaganda in ancient times, and the first author in history, Priestess Enheduanna, is a very good example of this. Her hymns and letters asserted that her father Sargon was the righteous ruler of the Akkadian Empire, and she made the cult of the moon god Nanna and his daughter Inanna central to the empire.

Although the goddess Inanna is a very early example of syncretism with other goddesses (Asher-Greve 2013, 43), I demonstrate in the chapter "The Lady of the Sea" that she later became equated with Ishtar because of Enheduanna. Most myths are political schemes that assert, explain, and implement a new religious order. A good example of that is the numerous tales of Zeus taking over mortals and goddesses by rape.

The rape mythological pattern is an interesting topic here. Rape by divine gods can symbolize many things, especially societal and personal change and even death. Greek and Roman societies, especially from the fifth century BCE, were very strict about what women could do; women had specific roles in society as daughters, wives, and mothers. Rape imagery was apparently popular on funerary steles in late antiquity and the rape stories could have been a symbolic narrative of the death of an old life and moving toward a new one: "The ancient Greeks believed that the transition period in the life of a woman, from puberty to maturity, was a form of metaphorical death and apotheosis. This transition period in the life of a woman, symbolically manifested in Europa or in Kore, was also present in Roman funerary art. Europa's adventure illustrates the 'rite of passage'" (Pilipović 2001, 67). The rape story would represent here, according to this thesis, the passage from maidenhood to womanhood. It was apparently compared to the death of the body and the travel of the soul into another life, hence the use of this motif for funerary purposes. Based on how, before the Greeks, some myths explained religious change by gods killing other gods, I see Zeus as a figure of the political and religious change that came about by the time he appears in the Greek pantheon around the first millennium BCE. Sexual submission or rape could also represent power that is taken from the victim—such as when a cult replaced a god or goddess with another. As such, myths cannot be the only source for understanding ancient religions, as they can mean so many different things and they do not reflect the private practices of common people. Folklore and archaeological finds, coupled with myths and historical texts, can send us toward a better understanding of the ancient mind.

To briefly summarize the relationships the ancients seemed to have had with the astral world, here are some patterns I observed through many ancient cultures: The moon, especially the crescent moon, was often a male deity but in fact he almost always had a female consort, but this consort was forgotten or misinterpreted. The same happened to Anu, a main male sky god; he had a consort named Antu, but you never hear of her. This means that the day sky was male and the night sky, female. The lunar female consort figure represented the full moon and sometimes the dark moon. The ancient female goddesses were also very often solar figures, and we only see the resurgence of a popular moon goddess later in the Classical Greek culture and the Roman periods. But I will discuss how she probably was always there, just not understood properly. Venus is always understood as a dual-gender divinity because this planet appears both in the evening and the morning as the first and last visible "star." Therefore lore and festivals integrate the very complex nature of this celestial object (Kasak and Veede, 22–24).

In the Sumerian world, there was a goddess for everything; for example, beer, seen as a magic potion to aid in women's health, was guarded by the goddess Ninkasi. The creatrix of the gods and the weavers of life were goddesses as well. The scribes and the guardians of the underworld were goddesses. The healing and dream oracular beings were goddesses. Sex and desire was also a goddess. Finally, goddesses were very often the deities who guarded cities and provided warriors with their fighting spirit. That demonstrates that almost every important sphere of life was thought to be under the rule of a feminine power (Asher-Greve 2013), although I am cautious about the word *feminine*, as divine gender cannot be understood from our modern point of view (Stavrakopoulou 2017).

The Bronze Age

The Bronze Age was undeniably a multicultural era characterized by remarkable innovations. Emphasizing this aspect is crucial in comprehending the transformation, adaptation, and disappearance of certain gods and goddesses within specific cultural spheres. It is also fascinating to note that during the Bronze Age and Iron Age, nearly every culture shared a similar understanding of the world. While this assumption is significant, archaeological evidence from pre–Bronze Age periods provides clues supporting this notion. However, a shift in religious concepts becomes apparent toward the end of the Bronze Age. During this period, civilizations increasingly prioritized masculine ideals but not as much as the Classical era. The collapse of Bronze Age Mediterranean cultures in 1200 BCE led to a dark age for a time. Despite this, little changed in the popular religion of ordinary people, who continued to worship many goddesses.

The Syro-Mesopotamian Religious World

The cuneiform literature informs us that the Sumerians understood their roles as human beings as existing only to serve the gods. However, they also did care deeply about their loved ones, had a heightened sense of justice, and cared for the nature around them. They were already nostalgic for a lost golden age. In this mythical narrative it was believed that humans lived for centuries and peace was prevalent everywhere. This narrative is common in humanity and stems from a possible collective unconscious sense of wanting to return to the origins, which Mircea Eliade described in his work *The Myth of the Eternal Return*.

Five thousand years ago, the first people who expressed themselves in writing shared the same worries as we do today. This is what ancient history always teaches us: that our ancestors were not that different, and that humanity has always had the same issues and dreams. The Sumerians' religion, like all religions in antiquity, was mostly animistic (Perdibon 2019). New research among scholars confirms more and more that the Bronze Age worldview was closer to what we find in modern indigenous cultures. That means that gods and goddesses were nonhuman beings emanating from nature itself. They were linked to specific places in the natural world, such as a river, tree, or cave, and those topographical features would be named after them. You had an Inanna of Uruk and an Inanna of Isin, for example. The most important features in their religion were the stars and planets. The constellations were called the writings of the heavens. The very dark night sky in antiquity was certainly impressive. The myriad of sparkling eyes in the sky looking down on humans made them think the stars were god-like guardians watching over them.

The other sacred spaces of the Mesopotamian world were the waters, springs, groves, and mountains (Perdibon 2019). Their temples, called ziggurats, were intended to connect, at their highest point, with the sky and the divinities. The winds also held religious importance for the Syro-Mesopotamians. One of their greatest gods, Enlil, lord of the winds, was a powerful being. The Syro-Mesopotamians saw winds as a liminal power. Ninlil, the goddess of the air and wind, was the main goddess of destiny and mother of the moon. The winds were linked to different cardinal directions, and as such they were linked to the movements of the stars. South winds, for example, were thought to bring evil diseases and was the abode of demons (Wiggerman). The Syro-Mesopotamians believed that the stars and other heavenly bodies controlled humanity's destiny and that no escape was possible. The only recourse was to ask certain goddesses to intercede for you when you thought a god was angry with you. This was certainly the case in ancient Mesopotamia and in the surrounding cultures of the Bronze Age, as shown in magical literature.

But astral religion is perhaps the least understood feature of ancient religions because of the anthropomorphic images of the deities scholars have found. For most of us, the mainstream Western Christian culture has modeled how we perceive and relate to religions. We understand deities to be invisible human-like gods, whereas the ancients understood them as energetic emanations that could be hosted in statues and other objects for specific purposes. In South India, astral magic is still practiced, with the powers of the stars and planets transposed into statues and amulets, just like in ancient times (Pingree 1989). Astrotheology is indeed still very much alive in this world.

The Anatolian Religious World

The Mediterranean world owes a lot to the great kingdoms that ruled over the land that is now Turkey. Anatolia had one of the greatest cultural influences over ancient Europe, although its own cultural identity seems to have been influenced by the Syro-Mesopotamian world. One of the biggest cultures was the Hittite kingdom, which rose during the Middle Bronze Age. Its culture was also very oriented toward the celestial world, particularly the moon, as many festivals were held for it (Zangger and Gautschy). Magic, spells, and necromancy were also used in correlation with the stars. Most male gods seemed to have been related to aspects of nature, such as storms, and goddesses were important figures for royalty. Being at first a nomadic culture that came from farther East, the Hittites gladly took over the Mesopotamian religions of their neighbors as their own but adapted them. Most of their sacred sites were in mountains, where we find rock carvings and a lot of astral references. These symbolic carvings provided entrance to the underworld where their sun goddess lived. They too left behind a rich literature that informs us of their spiritual life.

The Egyptian Religious World

In ancient Egypt, the religious system was very complex and well structured. Art was a big part of their religious expression. Because art was a sacred duty, artists and architects had to follow a well-established tradition. Iconographies were considered alive in themselves; they were vessels of the divine. As such, every construction, painting, and writing had to be perfect. Each painted figure had to be created in harmony and with precision or else its spirit would be stuck in an alternate reality. Every image had to be accompanied by a hieroglyphic text, which would confirm what the image was.

Just like in Mesopotamia, temples were very important. They were houses of the divine and represented the orderly cosmos. As such, temples had to be protected at all costs. The pyramids, as funerary tombs for the kings, were meant to stand for eternity, housing the spirit of the deceased. The pharaohs made certain they would live eternally by having their names and images engraved on these monumental symbols of eternal life. When a pharaoh's name is written in a sacred language and his portrait is fixed into eternity, he never ceases to exist. A pharaoh, when crowned, was transformed into a god, the son of the sun (Amun-Rê). This legitimacy is expressed through art. Through art, the myths surrounding the immortality of the king are narrated.

The king being suckled by a goddess legitimates that he was the son of a god and goddess and therefore has every right as a god himself to govern humans (Stuckey 2003). The sacred role of the kings in antiquity was embodied to make sure that the cosmos would stay in order and balance. Only the king as a divine messenger could ensure his kingdom was kept in peace. Any failure to this duty was an offense to sacredness. If you offended the gods and goddesses, then you would surely receive plagues, famines, and wars. Just like in Mesopotamia, Egypt had to ensure that the divinities were satisfied with the work of the kings or pharaohs.

The sacred powers that went into writing and art were directly drawn from the sky. Egyptians too understood that the powers of the divine came from the cosmos and that it was only by maintaining balance in the cosmos that immortality and peace could be achieved. This is exactly the concept of Maat, the cosmic order. This order, the Maat, is embodied by the goddess of the same name. The ancient Egyptian divinities were embodiments of the sacred stars, planets, and constellations. You can find traces of that perception in Nut, the goddess of the night sky; Amenti, the goddess who would receive and feed the deceased in the underworld; or Mut, the day sky goddess.

Finally, the ancient Egyptians had very elaborate conceptions about the afterlife. Whereas in Mesopotamia the deceased would just go live in the underworld forever, the Egyptians thought that there was a good afterlife for the just and suffering for the cruel. Because they believed in life after death, souls were also thought to reincarnate if need be. This is a major difference from the more pessimistic conceptions of Egypt's neighbors. This difference in afterlife beliefs explains why the cult of the ancestors was especially important to the Mesopotamians: the more sacrifice and honors you gave to the spirits of your family, the less chance they would disappear into oblivion.

The Ancient Greek Religious World

The ancient Greek religious world is fascinating because there is still much to discover about pre-Classical Greece. Minoan and Mycenaean cultures, for example, are the oldest we know of in the land we call

Greece today. But since their scripts are only partially deciphered, we do not know everything. Linear B, used by the Mycenaeans after the Minoan culture faded, tells us a few things, such as the names of deities and important kingdoms. Just from archaeological records, we know that the Minoans were trading with Eastern cultures, such as Cyprus, Egypt, and Syria, and that they were animistic or presented some shamanistic features in their religious practices (Tully and Crooks 2015). There seemed to have been sanctuaries in the mountain peaks, and the female figure seemed to have had an important place in their religious world. Images on their frescoes and painted pottery and their sculpture tell us that Minoans had a connection with bulls, trees, bees, the sea, and flowers. As such, they are seen as peaceful artisans who also practiced an interesting sport—bull leaping.

As for the Mycenaeans, they were quite different people. They were more militaristic, as were their deities. Mycenaeans had less nudity in their art than neighboring Eastern cultures, and their main goddess seemed to have been Potnia, the mistress of animals. Of course, the development of the Archaic period in Greece has seen various ancient rites. The Eleusinian mysteries, for example, are thought to have begun during this phase. This very ancient rite continued for centuries and was meant to prepare people for the afterlife. It was an ancient Greek ritual mimicking death and resurrection, although we do not know exactly how this ritual was done.

Archaic Greece left us records of other ancient rites, such as important rites of passage with Artemis or even with the mother of the gods, Cybele. It is important to note that a lot of ancient Greek gods were imported from the East, which means that the classical pantheon that we know about are a mix of indigenous gods and important deities that came from neighboring cultures (Bonnet et al. 2022). It's also important to understand that we see in the religious worldview of ancient Greece a shift in the social structure of males and females. Women had less and less power, which became very apparent in the Classical and Hellenistic periods. We can assume that before the deities became symbols of cities and civilization, that ancient Greece too had a peaceful relationship with nature and had an animistic worldview. The astral world was also something important in their spiritual life, and they even transformed the Babylonian astrological system into the zodiac we know today (Barton 1994).

The Etruscans and the Roman Religious World: The End of It All?

The Roman religious world shaped and transformed most of the ancient religions. It is, after all, under Roman rule that Christianity became a formal religion. Although the deities and magic texts that I studied and that provide the basis for this book are far older than the Roman period, I want to summarize the general conceptions of the world and the divine in ancient Etruria and in the Roman culture that followed.

First, the Etruscans are believed to have inhabited the territories of Italy before the arrival and conquest of the peoples who would later come to be known as the Romans. The Etruscans' iconographies shared similarities with Archaic Greece, as their culture arose during the first millenium BCE. Little is known of their actual religious views because there are more archaeological data than written data. Still, they have left some books, mostly about divination practices. Like their Eastern companions, they relied heavily on celestial divination (Johnston 2007).

Their divinities, like other ancient cultures, were deeply rooted to specific locations. The many divinities bore many names because each divinity represented the energy felt within a specific space. Not only did each city have its unique divinities but also each household and each person in the household. From ancient Mesopotamia to ancient Rome, it was widely believed that each human had personal spirits or gods with whom he or she had to maintain a relationship. We see the importance of the family spirit in the daily rituals of the ancient Romans, which translated into Catholicism. Still today, Roman Catholics celebrate the spirits of many saints, just like in the Roman Empire.

Along with their location-specific deities, the Etruscan people also adopted many Greek deities and even Eastern ones (Bonnet et al. 2022). Their goddess Uni, for example, was the Phoenician Astarte, patron goddess of Pyrgy in today's Tuscany. Her dedicated temple was oriented toward the southeast, following the cyclical changes of the seasons. Etruscans were therefore no strangers to the heavenly stars, and their importance is reflected in the orientation of their temples and their openness to the sky to receive celestial irradiation, the process of absorbing energy from the stars. We return to this concept in the last chapter, "Celestial Healing."

The Etruscans venerated sacred springs and lakes, mountains, and trees, just like their Mesopotamian neighbors (Bonnet et al. 2022). When the Romans arrived in Etruria, they thought the religions of the Etruscans were strange, but they allowed them to continue some cult activities. The Romans eventually became stricter in regulating religious activities, and numerous festivals were soon lost to time. The imposition of the imperial Roman religion, as well as the later arrival of the Christian faith, which became Rome's national religion, soon changed the religions of the ancient world for the next centuries. Still, some practices remained, expressed through the new religion or existing outside it. We can still see glimpses of the ancient world in the folk cults of Ireland, for example, who were left untouched by the Roman religions. The animistic worldview of the ancient Celtic peoples remains in Catholic local folklore. Although a very superstitious culture, the Romans were among the first to condemn the practice of what they perceived as malevolent magic.

THE ANCIENT ASTRAL RELIGIONS

Our modern culture is still imbued with the ancestral knowledge that the stars were divine. In our day-to-day language and beliefs, we use this star language without noticing what it really means, with old sayings like: "It's written in the stars," "Aim for the stars," "Born under a lucky star," or even "The stars are aligned." These lingering sayings demonstrate ancient human beliefs that our fates and lives are entwined with the stars. I am not even mentioning how astrology is still very present in our culture. We still, whether we really believe in it or not, give importance to the astrological signs of a person.

Evidently, even with the rise of Christianity, the beliefs and practices of ancient Western Asia were not lost overnight. For example, a sect of the Sabian people, a religious group mentioned in the Quran, kept their worship of the stars until the twelfth century. Slavic people, even though they did not write, were also not converted to Christianity until the eleventh century and maintained their worship of gods and goddesses and the astral realm. Ancient astral magic survived through the medieval period to early modern times in occult magical texts from Arabic and other Eastern cultures. The Jewish culture, which inherited astral beliefs from Mesopotamia, has kept some ancient magic knowledge about the stars in its texts, which has been used by different esoteric movements throughout history. Today, there are many people who still use this ancient magic through amulets and stones. These are mostly various groups who follow the left-hand path in Western esotericism.

In Eastern European cultures, some archaic folklore seems to parallel the ancient Mesopotamian and Persian cultures: Some of the names the ancient Slavic people gave to the constellations is the same or similar to those of the Mesopotamians. As an example, in ancient Slavic culture, Ursa Major is called the Wagon, which is exactly how the Mesopotamian people referred to this constellation. The following quote from Olga Stanton shows how the ancient Slavs were very similar to the ancient Mediterranean and Mesopotamian people in how they viewed heavenly bodies.

Slavs viewed stars and planets that could be seen in the night sky as living creatures that were born, lived, glimmering in the sky and sometimes moving from place to place (comets, asteroids, and meteors), bathed, slept, "talked," and died. Sometimes, our ancestors viewed them as fair maidens that fly in the sky, holding candles or burning splinters in their hands. They dance, circle around in, and play hide-and-seek. This is why the position of stars in the sky is not always the same. All stars serve to Deities: morning and day stars serve to Zimtserla, aka Zarya-Zaryanitsa; evening and night stars are controlled by the Dark, nighttime Deities. In Southern Slavic and Belarussian mythology, stars are a silvery veil that adorns the head of the sky. By counting them one can tell how many living souls there are in the world: once a baby is born, his or her star is lit, once a person dies, the star goes out. Bright stars belong to world's leaders: princes (knyazya), tsars, or kings; small and dull ones belong to poor and unlucky people, and the smallest ones belong to animals: wild and domestic, birds and fishes. However, one should not rush to search for his or her star—if a man identifies his star in the sky, he would die soon. Counting the stars or even pointing at them was also a bad idea, because this is how a man could accidentally find his star.*

This lore living in the deep consciousness of humans refers to many symbols we find in the ancient world. Goddess statues often wore elements that refer to the celestial world and its lights. For example, they sometimes held candles and wore veils, crowns, and jewels—all this represents their celestial nature. Indeed, the skies were often referred to as having veils, as illustrated in the preceding quote.

This celestial world was of major importance for every ancient culture. Not only were the stars and planets gods, but the omens they sent were of importance to kings. Astrology developed in the Near East, and the stars, seen as messages from the gods, could foretell if days were auspicious or inauspicious. The Babylonians further developed astrological divination in the second and first millennia, and omens were eventually applied to all people, not just kings. The democratization of writing and reading among ancient societies made astrological knowledge available for everyone, and the predictions written in the skies, originally meant only for the kings, became available to all. Still, it was an art and science that very few priests could master. The ancient kingdom of Elam (Iran) developed astrology and astronomy possibly before Sumer. We have indeed names of constellations that are said to have originated from the kingdom of Elam. Sumerians then adopted this system into their own. The same thing eventually happened with the Greeks. The Greeks first adopted astronomical knowledge from the Babylonians and Hittites and then developed their own astrological system, which developed further during the medieval period and eventually became modern astrology (Barton 1994).

*Olga Stanton via the Facebook page "MagPie's Corner—East Slavic Rituals, Witchcraft and Culture," accessed January 1, 2023.

To assess how the celestial bodies were of importance in everyday ancient cults and medicine, I have included a prayer, called "prayers to the gods of the night," that is very useful and telling of the powers that hold the planets and constellations. This prayer, dating from the Old Babylonian period (1894–1595 BCE), is thought to be the work of a diviner that asks for help from the deities to get an answer to his question.

> The nobles are deep in sleep, the bars of the doors are lowered, the bolts(?) are in place—(also) the (ordinary) people do not utter a sound, the(ir always) open doors are locked. The gods and goddesses of the country—Samas, Sin, Adad and Istar—have gone home to heaven to sleep, they will not give decisions or verdicts (tonight) May the great gods of the night: shining Fire-star, heroic Irra, Bow-star, Yoke-star, Orion, Dragon-star, Wagon, Goat-star, Bison-star, Serpent-star stand by and put a propitious sign in the lamb I am blessing now for the haruspicy I will perform (at dawn). (Reiner 1995,1)

This formula invokes the important gods but also constellations and even the fire spirit. It was believed, like the text mentions, that the gods were asleep in their temples, but that the stars were looking down at us during the night. The deities in ancient religions had a dual and even triple nature. For example, the sun was seen as masculine during the day, being the judge of every day, but feminine during the dawn and sunset, as leader of the underworld at night. The animistic view of ancient religions also assigned great importance to the elements of nature surrounding us (Perdibon 2019). During the Bronze Age, the Mesopotamian and Mediterranean worlds were mountainous and full of forests. It was believed that mountains were gates to the underworld and that goddesses lived on mountaintops, as they were reaching toward the sky. This is the same reason that Mesopotamian ziggurats, Egyptian pyramids, and Hittite temples were built high with an apex that was as close as possible to the heavens. The physical manifestation of the deities resided at the top of these structures.

Water was also considered a portal to another world. For example, water was known to be in the underworld, so to give an offering to the waters was to ensure that your intent would reach the gods. Water was also seen as a mirror reflecting the celestial bodies, therefore the saying "as above, so below" was already a concept well understood in antiquity, although they may not have said it exactly like that. You could reach your deity by giving your prayers or incantations to the waters reflecting the sun, the stars, or the moon, a very efficient way to make sure you would be heard. Therefore, all the great goddesses, the queens of the heavens and Earth, were patrons of the heavens, seas, and underworld, and these planes of existence were interconnected. These associations, based on observations of the world, were quite logical, when we think about it.

Lesser spirits were known to inhabit trees and plants; they were understood as mediators between the worlds. In the Bronze Age, trees were already a symbol of connection between the three planes: the underworld, the human world, and the sky. The essence and nature of multiple types of wood were thought to have specific powers, and therefore wood was used to make physical representations of the deities. As the sky was regarded with sacred reverence, the ancients understood how to harness the power of the stars. This is how magic and medicine became intertwined as a manifestation of cosmic consciousness. This power could be harnessed into statues made of wood or stone. Precious metals, which were understood to represent the physical nature of the stars, were used as amulets. I like to quote anthropologist Philippe Descola (2020) about this when he says, "La nature n'existe pas," translated as "Nature does not exist." What he means is that we invented the concept of nature as something separate from us, nature versus culture. In his work he demonstrates that naturalism, as an invention of the "Siècle des lumières," cuts us humans from our very nature, which is that we are part of the ecosystem, as our ancestors understood it. We were never apart from nature and never will be; we are nature and as such we should maintain a good relationship with other nonhumans (Descola 2005).

CELESTIAL CELEBRATIONS

Every culture had many festivals linked to a specific deity and to the constellation or star associated with that deity. Tracking the movements of celestial objects was an important practice in agriculture. Today, many farmers still use the phases of the moon and cyclical movements in constellations for their crops. The stars were not just for agriculture but also served as an important navigation tool for sailors. The rising and setting of a star was also a navigational signal for hunters in nomadic societies who did not use agriculture. As such, celebration of the rising of specific stars and the changing of seasons has always been important for humanity. Since there were many such celebrations, I will simply present those celebrations regarding constellations that were similar in the various cultures of the ancient world. It is not simple to assess because the astronomical dates were not fixed. Ancient people followed a lunar calendar, and because of that, the dates of rising and setting stars were never the same.

The Babylonians are widely credited with developing the first calendars, marking the beginning of time as a quantifiable concept. They employed a 360-day year, consisting of twelve lunar months of thirty days each. They also established a seven-day week, corresponding to the four phases of the lunar cycle. The ancient Egyptians adopted the Babylonian twelve-month calendar as well. This calendar system was used until it was changed in 46 BCE to the Julian calendar during the Roman Empire, and then in the Middle Ages, the Western world adopted the Gregorian calendar, which we still use today.

At least six major celebrations were common in the ancient world.

☽ **The celebration of the spring planting and the fall harvest.** Today's modern pagans recognize these dates as Imbolc, the beginning of spring celebrated on February 1, and Lammas or Lughnasadh, which celebrates the fall harvest beginning on August 1. These celebrations corresponded to the festivals of important goddesses such as the Assyrian goddess Atargatis and the Sumerian goddess Inanna.

☽ **Orion and the winter and summer solstices.** These were major festivals in every culture to mark the coming of these two major seasons, which were considered dangerous in ancient times. In winter, less food was available and it was the season of death, and in summer, the scorching heat could kill the crops and dry the water sources. Solstice festivals were the main rituals associated with the goddesses of death.

Being very visible in the winter sky, from November to February, Orion has many associations with the winter solstice. In ancient times the three stars in Orion's belt were known as the Three Kings or the Three Mages. In other cultures, they are referred to as the Three Marys or the Magician's Staff. The setting of Orion in February is connected to other festivals honoring the lands of the dead and the healing powers of goddesses. This can be seen in Europe through the celebrations of the goddess Brigit and other female spirits who have powers over the dead and regeneration.

☽ **Pleiades festivals.** Since Pleiades means "doves," there is a very good chance that this constellation of seven stars was associated with celebrations of the dead (Haliburton 1920), as will be discussed in another chapter. The Sumerians saw the Pleiades as a crown of seven flames on the goddess Inanna, and she, too, is connected to the dead realm (Konstantopoulos 2015). The seven stars were often considered protectors of the ancestors' realm. In many cultures the disappearance of the Pleiades in November and its association with the bull of heaven is linked to ancient dead festivals and also to renewal in the cult of Isis and Osiris, as the growing season in Egypt began in mid-November (Haliburton 1920). In every culture you will find stories about the Pleiades, very often called the Seven Sisters. In Italy they were the nymphs Electra, Maia, Taygete, Alcyone, Celaeno, Sterope, and Merope (Tzetz. *ad Lyc.* 219, comp. 149; Apollod. iii. 10. § 1). In ancient Mesopotamia, the Pleiades were powerful demons that could be helpful to kings or be destructive; because the stars were always moving, their energies were considered unstable (Konstantopoulos 2015). From being demons, to sages, to nymphs, the myths surrounding the Pleiades have made their way to us.

There are of course many more important stars and constellations also related to the many other male gods. Since the focus of this book is goddesses, I chose not to explore all the details of ancient astronomy and celestial celebrations, but you can find very good sources if you want to learn more.*

As noted earlier, I have divided the celestial goddesses into four major categories and have devoted a chapter to each category or typology: the creatrix, the warrior, the healer, and the lady of the sea. In the next chapter, I present the solar underworld goddesses and the figure of the creatrix, who is related to the Milky Way. Next, I present the maiden warrior, who often works with the solar aspect and the eagle symbol. Then we explore the infamous goddesses linked to death and healing powers with the night sky. Finally, I present the lady of the sea and her transformative powers. I have included, for those interested, an introduction to ancient celestial rituals in the last chapter, "Celestial Healing: Rituals for Reconnecting with the Stellar Goddesses."

---

*I recommend *Astral Magic in Babylonia* by Erica Reiner and *Calendars and Festivals in Mesopotamia in the Third and Second Millennia BC*, edited by Daisuke Shibata and Shigeo Yamada.

Mentr' el tuo Padre in quella, en questa parte
Seguish o' Roma, e' mentre' i membri uniti
Tenesti del tuo corpo, ognun di Marte'
T'aueua per figlia e' trionfando i siti

Tuoi d'abbondantia empisti, e' tal fu l'arte'
Che' ne' trabocco' l teuere ei sue' liti:
Gran segni ancor nel uentre' tuo si uede'
Che gia tenesti 'l mondo sotto' l piede'

ANT. SAL: EXC.

Cybele in Her Chariot Drawn by Two Lions, print by Master of the Die, after
Baldassare Tommaso Peruzzi, sixteenth century (Metropolitan Museum of Art)

THE CREATRIX

The Eye Goddess, Ninhursag and Hathor,
Neith and Nut, Kubaba, Sun Goddess of
Arinna, Shapash, Asherah, Allat

. . . .

Celestial Bodies: Sun, Milky Way
Symbols: Owl, lion, trees, stones, weaving
Season: The dark season (winter)
Symbolic Message: Rebirth

. . . .

O my mother Nut, spread yourself over me, so that I may be placed among the imperishable stars and may never die . . . that my name might remain enduring in this temple forever and ever.

QUEEN HATSHEPSUT

In this chapter, I introduce the goddesses associated with the dark season of wintertime. Although all goddesses are in one way or another related to the night and darkness, the creatrix solar figures were especially celebrated during winter solstice and the dark season. In this symbolic scheme, the creatrix is a figure who brings forth life but who also represents all the dangers of the dark season. As such, these goddesses needed to be appeased and celebrated. Many festivals and celebrations for the creatrix energies were linked to funerals and conquering the fear of death.

Under their many forms, the mothers of the cosmos take us back home to the stars when we depart this world. As our bodies, which are made of the same matter as the stars, return to the Earth, our spark of energy surely goes back to this cosmic family, which we belong to. It is still

29

mysterious how our ancestors knew this, but clearly their intuition was in tune with the world. They knew that we belonged to the stars. They gave great power to the figures that symbolized the "mother" in the sky or the solar psychopomp goddess who guides souls.

As such, there is no harder topic to explore than that of the ancient mother of the gods, the creatrix. Found in many cultures, the roles of these creatrixes evolved through time. In this chapter I will treat different aspects of the deities we called mothers of the gods and demonstrate that the sun goddess of the Mediterranean was quite important in relation to this role. Those divine figures were seen as mothers in the sense that they were the creatrix energies associated with the solar power and the night sky. Most of the time, these goddesses were understood as the vital force that gave birth to the cosmos. They are not to be understood as literal mothers of humans or even fertility goddesses. Their work was related to death and rebirth, especially, and sometimes protection of women in labor and dying children. We must not forget that the dangers of pregnancy were very real and the infant death rate was high, and therefore mothers-to-be and newborns needed more protection. The great power and symbolism of these sacred figures have persisted through time and history. Today, she is coming back under various cults.

In the ancient Mediterranean world, numerous revered figures embodied the concepts discussed. One such figure is the goddess Eileithyia from Crete, widely worshipped throughout Greece for her association with childbirth, eventually becoming linked with Artemis and Hecate. Additionally, these figures were often skilled weavers, with spinning and weaving activities symbolizing the protection of women and the essence of life itself. They were deeply intertwined with the worship of sacred trees and stones, symbolic of winter and the underworld. We will delve into how these mother figures, connected to the Milky Way's pattern, were perceived as guardians of life, while also being revered as the sun goddesses of the Earth, embodying the duality of life and death. An important aspect to note is that these underworld goddesses were sometimes worshipped as a triad, often bearing different names but sharing core attributes.

An example highlighting the connection between these triple mother figures and the winter solstice celebration is found in the writings of the medieval monk Bede. He mentions an Anglo-Saxon (Germanic) observance called "Mothers' Night," held on the eve of the winter solstice to honor a form of the three Matronae, representing ancestral fate spirits. Although Bede's account is the only source documenting this practice, it likely emerged due to the widespread association of the dark season with creatrix and fate goddesses.

Contemporary Death and Dying

We live in a society that is very scared of aging and dying. Aging is especially difficult for women, as society dictates how women should look, and women feel pressure to stay looking as young as possible, fearful they will end up alone and lonely. When the goddesses were forgotten, Western culture was left with primarily male gods, including positive archetypes for older men—the old, bearded man and loving father. Consequently, men tend to be less scared about getting old. Everyone, however, must face death, which modern Western culture has pushed away. Understanding and reclaiming the ancient wisdom of the goddesses can help us heal our relationship with the cycle of death and rebirth.

In contemporary cultures we can still find solar goddesses, such as the Japanese Amaterasu or the Scandinavian Sol; in fact sun goddesses were numerous. But in Mediterranean cultures, those very same cultures that heavily influenced the Western world, we are used to understanding the sun as a male figure such as Helios, Apollo, or Horus. The solar goddess of the Mediterranean world was an underworld goddess. With the coming of night, the sun was observed sinking below the horizon, apparently disappearing behind Earth (Collins 2014, 225). For the ancients, that meant that the sun was living in the underworld at night. Her infernal aspect was therefore a focus in her cult, as will be explored. Over time, some cultures challenged the status identity of the sun as being female because the importance status of the women had changed in those cultures; they had lost power. Changes in religions and interpretations of the divine figures can indicate and help us understand the societal changes that happened during that period.

Today, the energy of the creatrix is talking to us very loudly. As the sacred tree of life that connects the Earth with the heavenly forces of the

Milky Way, which is our final resting place, she calls for us to reconnect and protect the very nature that made us. She is the type of divine energy that guides you through dark moments, helps in your healing, and answers prayers. Even today, sacred sites associated with the Virgin Mary or female saints receive many offerings from people searching for help and peace.

THE EYE GODDESS

The eye goddess, known as the all-seeing deity, holds a significant place as one of the oldest divine entities and a recurring motif in ancient cultures. Serving as a potent symbol of mystical safeguarding, the eye carries a rich spiritual legacy. Often regarded as the windows to the soul, eyes embody profound meanings, and various superstitions surrounding them persist to this day. Protective blue eye talismans, designed to ward off malevolence and hexes, are widely available across the Mediterranean region, serving as tangible symbols of safeguarding. In regions like Turkey, Greece, Israel, and Lebanon, eyes held profound magical significance, intertwined with cultural beliefs and practices. The hand of Fatima, featuring a protective eye within its palm, remains a cherished amulet in Muslim societies across North Africa and the Middle East. This belief system finds its roots in the ancient Phoenician trade networks that spanned vast distances. The notion of the evil eye, casting malevolent influences upon individuals, originates from the fear of attracting envy due to one's success in life, which could potentially lead to curses and misfortune. Envy, thus, has long been viewed as a malevolent force in various cultural contexts.

In ancient art, it is not uncommon to come across abstract figures that primarily feature eyes, suggesting that these objects may have served as magical amulets. Recently, such artifacts were discovered in the northern Levant, a region in the Eastern Mediterranean of West Asia, specifically at the site known as Newe Yam (Galili, Kolska-Horwitz, and Rosen 2015). These amulets, carved from bone, date back to 8000 BCE and depict some of the earliest known iconography of a possible eye goddess. Interestingly, these figures have been found not only in the Levant but also as far as the Iberian Peninsula (Schuhmacher 2013). Archaeologists have found many of these figures in tombs alongside what appear to be idols with solar eye features, resembling bird-like faces. The presence of these potential goddesses in tombs suggests that ancient people relied on their protective energy in the afterlife, particularly for the safeguarding of young children. Notably, a significant number of these images were discovered in children's tombs. This indicates the belief in providing protection in the afterlife through these amulets.

Several thousand years later, we can still discover comparable artwork originating from the fourth millennium BCE in Anatolia, Syria, and even Spain. The figures found in Spain bear a striking resemblance to those of the Levant and are believed to represent a solar goddess associated with ancestral worship and death rituals. This ancient deity appears to have been interpreted as the same divine force across various cultures, as evidenced by the shared iconography. The eyes of these figures are often surrounded by rays and resemble an owl. The owl was commonly associated with death, believed to be the carrier of the departed soul. It is worth noting the similarities between these goddesses and the renowned Tell Brak eye idols from the fourth millennium, located in Syria. The little eye idols have been interpreted as being eye goddesses or even as a weaving tool (Cooper 2016). On the same site, at Tell Brak in Syria, there was a temple dedicated to the life-giving Sumerian goddess Ninhursag. It is very possible that these eye figures are related to a proto-Ninhursag goddess (Steinkeller 1994, 983). This potential proto-Ninhursag deity carried symbols relating to eyes, mountains, wild animals, and the sun—telling silent stories embedded in motifs that would later become universal.

The powerful creatrix Ninhursag was later replaced, in most of her temples, by the popular goddess Inanna. A stelae found in a Syrian temple with similar owl eyes could be the origin of the foliage and deer symbolism found later in the Mediterranean world, mostly on amulets (Steinkeller 1994, 983). As such, the owl imagery is often related to the goddesses of the underworld and death cults.

In ancient Egyptian beliefs, the eye goddess was the daughter of the sun god Ra. The Egyptians referred to the sun and the moon as the eyes of the sky god. Maat, the Egyptian goddess of truth and cosmic balance, personified this eye of Ra, and sometimes other important goddesses related to death such as Bastet and Hathor also appeared in art as the eye of Ra. The right eye was believed to be more protective, but the left eye was used to send curses to enemies (Darnell 1997).

These eye goddesses, or idols, described previously, also resemble owls or possibly represent another type of bird of prey. Since they have been in the Mediterranean world since at least the sixth millennium in Anatolia and around, these are maybe the earliest attestation of a death and rebirth goddess such as Ninhursag and maybe even a proto-Athena (Yilmaz 2016). The underworld solar cults and owl figures are very often linked, in the ancient world, with cults to the ancestors. Spirits of the deceased were believed to live in the underworld after their death, and they could suffer from thirst and hunger. The care of the deceased was extremely important. As such, lonely individuals who died from an untimely death or without rituals dedicated to them, would become ghosts or demons. In many very ancient tombs, the entrance would let the sun enter the chamber, so the goddess could find the souls and bring them to their final resting place.

Finally, very often the owl image is associated with lions. Lion is a royal and power symbol important for kings. Goddesses associated with owls and lions are for example the Mesopotamian Queen of the underworld Ereshkigal. You can also find the owl lore in the Arabian tales of the owl as death and afterlife guardian (Homerin 1985).

NINHURSAG AND HATHOR

The mother of the gods bore many names. One of her epithets in Mesopotamia was Ninhursag, possibly meaning the "one who dwells in mountains." Her main known symbol is omega, the last letter in the Greek alphabet, and scholars do not know what it signifies. Since the goddess was thought to be a midwife goddess, it has been suggested that the omega symbol represents a uterus. This, in my opinion, is a very reductive interpretation. When the goddess is present in medical and healing scenes depicted in art, the omega symbol that represents her is located in the sky near the sun and the moon. Although we lost the meaning of this symbol, it could have been the representation of a celestial phenomenon such as the Milky Way. Indeed the brightest nebulae in the Milky Way is the Omega

S

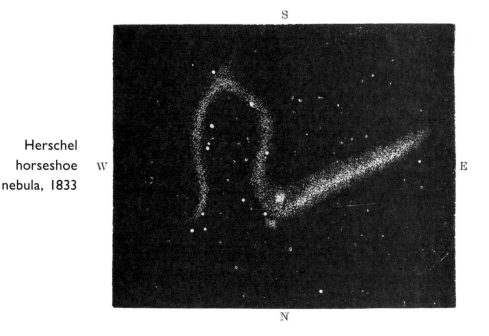

W

Herschel
horseshoe
nebula, 1833

E

N

Nebula, which is shaped like the omega letter or horseshoe, as illustrated by astronomer Herschel in 1833 (Holden 1876). That the creatrix Ninhursag could possibly be related to this nebula in the Milky Way seems like a wild suggestion, but it is supported by the fact that this nebula can be seen with the naked eye on the darkest nights of the winter. Therefore, it is possible that the ancients could see it more easily than we do today. This could also support the idea that creatrix goddesses are symbolic wintertime mothers.

One of the most intriguing aspects of the ancient omega symbol is its transformation into a hairstyle worn by various life-giving goddesses. The earliest instances of this hairstyle can be traced back to female figures from Elam and Sumer during the second millennium BCE (Bouillon 2014). Over time, this symbol found its way to the Egyptian goddess Hathor around 1200 BCE. Hathor, an esteemed Egyptian deity associated with magic and rebirth, shares many similarities with the Sumerian goddess Ninhursag. The connection between Ninhursag, Hathor, and the omega symbol linked to the Milky Way is notable in their roles within cult practices and ancient texts. Ninhursag's celestial nature is emphasized in Sumerian literature, describing her as "the true and great queen of heaven—when she talks heaven trembles, when she opens her mouth a storm thunders" (Black et al., 4.80.1: 96–97). This cosmic association is further highlighted by her role as a creatrix alongside Enki, the Sumerian god of water, magic, and wisdom. Together, they fashioned humankind and created the paradise garden of Dilmun, believed by scholars to have inspired the Garden of Eden story in Genesis. The cow symbolism associated with Ninhursag also hints at her celestial connection, as seen in prayers addressing her as the "Bride of Enki" and the "great wild cow." This symbolism, prevalent in ancient cultures, often refers to the Milky Way as the "milk of the goddess of life." Similarly, Hathor in Egypt was also depicted as a celestial cow, with horns adorned by stars, symbolizing the origin of life from the sky (Graves-Brown 2010). Both Ninhursag and Hathor were revered as celestial cows, overseeing human fates and the realms of souls within the Milky Way.

As previously mentioned, there is a belief that ancient astronomical stone circles were associated with the worship of Hathor by the Egyptians. She was so revered that cult leaders reportedly provided psychotropic substances to devotees, enabling them to commune with the goddess through visions and inducing euphoria (Graves-Brown 2010). However, this practice was not unique to the cult of Hathor, as other cultures also employed similar methods. Hathor, known for her affinity for music and dance, was worshipped in various ways, including through weaving and her association with the sycamore tree, and was often depicted in such contexts. The sycamore tree was a symbol of nourishment for the dead (Billing 2004). In Sumerian mythology, Ninhursag held a special connection with Uttu, who was both her daughter and a goddess of weaving. Interestingly, the cuneiform symbol used to represent Uttu's name also symbolized a spider, reflecting the strong association between weaving and fate in ancient cultures. This symbolism is evident in Sumerian art depicting spiders alongside women engaged in weaving and spinning, symbolizing the intricate weaving of human destinies by Uttu. Over time, Uttu became conflated with Inanna, leading to Inanna's emergence as a multiple-form goddess, known to have seven emanations. Similarly, Hathor also evolved into a sevenfold goddess, incorporating the roles and attributes of other deities.

NEITH AND NUT

Neith is one of the lesser known Egyptian goddesses but also one of the oldest. First mentions of her are found by the end of the fourth millennium BCE. Like any other very old goddesses, her original role was sometimes changed to assimilate other functions over time. Neith is seen originally as a goddess caring for the dead. Nut as the night sky goddess, mother of all the stars, was also a figure of protection in death. It was believed that the departed soul would join her in the Milky Way at the time of death. We can find depictions of Neith and Nut on a sarcophagus where Neith is shown accompanying the deceased to the land of Nut. Neith was also the goddess of warriors who died in battle and is herself a warrior and protector, depicted carrying a bow and arrows.

Great Neith was also a demiurge goddess, meaning she participated in creating the world. She was believed to have created the universe from the cosmic waters; as such, water was associated with her. As for Nut, she created the gods because she is the constellation that carries them, and through her the sun and the moon are reborn each morning. The pharaohs had prayers and hymns written to her on their sarcophagus, as they hoped to join the stars of Nut in the Milky Way when they died. As such, great Nut is the embodiment of the Milky Way, a starry world where the ancient Egyptians and others thought the souls would go after death. This imagery was represented in sarcophagus art to aid the transition of the departed.

According to another myth, Neith created the world by pronouncing seven words. The ancient world considered speech to be very powerful, which is why incantations and prayers are said out loud. The ancients thought speech created reality, and therefore in many ancient cosmologies, the gods created the world through speech. Spells are called spells because spelling them out loud creates reality. Because the cosmos is interconnected in a web of interaction, Neith was also a weaving goddess. She would weave destinies in tapestry, an art mastered by important women at that time. To see our lives as something that is woven through time is an important concept from the ancient world. They understood human lives as being part of the world, woven into the cosmos, one with the gods and other spirits.

In Greek myth, the figure of Arachne, who was a talented weaver, also relates to these ancient goddesses who wove the destinies of humans. Arachne was the daughter of a Phoenician trader, and therefore she could be a late survival of Uttu, the spider. She challenged Athena—who, among her various roles, was a weaving goddess and patron of the arts—to a weaving contest and was later transformed into a spider. This notion that the web of life is maintained by skillful goddesses, guardians of the dead in the Milky Way, is comforting and explains why goddesses had a prominent place in ancient cities and private cults. Male gods had other important functions, but people's lives were literally in the hands of goddesses.

KUBABA

In ancient Anatolian religions, whether of the Hittites or the Luwians, the goddess Kubaba was a guardian of the underworld. She appears with dark gods such as Šanta, thought to be servants in the underworld. The name Kubaba is therefore very often linked to protective spells and curses aimed at bandits who would disturb tombs. She is often depicted holding a large mirror. This suggests she is related to divination and communication with the dead. Necromancy, the act of speaking with the dead, very often used onyx mirrors in ancient times. Sometimes mirrors made of gold or other types of metal were used as well, as they directly reflected the sun goddess. Kubaba is thought to be the main influence for the goddess Cybele and Magna Mater, the great mother of the gods. She has a solar and chthonic aspect, meaning she too is related to a sun goddess of the underworld, keeper of the deceased. In Mesopotamia, the sun deity Shamash was female before changing to a male form (Asher-Greve 2013, 60). It is therefore not surprising that the sun as a female figure can be found in the Mediterranean world as well.

SUN GODDESS OF ARINNA

In Anatolia, more specifically in Arinna, an underworld solar entity was called the sun goddess of the Earth, because the sun is responsible for all life on this planet. This goddess of Arinna was also called the Great Torch and the Radiant One, highlighting the importance of her presence. This solar goddess is often depicted as a gold seated statue with a child on her lap. In the ancient world, the image of a child seated in a goddess's lap signaled the royal status of the child. In this way, major goddesses legitimated future kings, becoming their symbolic mothers. That this goddess is sitting on a throne is a good indicator of her powers. Let's not forget that the throne is also a symbol of the heavens. To better understand why there is a link between a sun goddess and the underworld, researcher Billie Jean Collins explained it in the context of understanding pit rituals, which are rituals I present in the last chapter: "She is a solar deity by virtue of representing the sun's cycle at night, after it dips below the horizon in the evening and before it rises again in the morning. Thus, rituals performed in order to communicate with her tend to occur at night, in the early morning, or the late evening." (Collins 2014, 224)

Major solar goddesses were known to give life or resurrect those who had died. The sun goddess of Arinna was responsible for protecting the king and the royal family; as such, many hymns were dedicated to her to prevent harm to the royals such as gossip and curses. Here is an example of a hymn showing how the sun goddess's powers were celebrated to acquire protection and health:

> Protect in the future the *labarna*, your priest, and your *tawannanna*, your priestess, together with his sons and his grandsons! Rejuvenate them and make them eternal!
> §9' (ii 27–36) Whoever are the *labarna's* first-rank people—his favored great ones, his infantry, his chariotry and their property—keep them, the aforementioned, alive in the hand of the *labarna* and the *tawannanna*, O most vigorous Sun-goddess! (Singer 2002, 26)

The sun goddess in Anatolia had varying roles. She was sometimes, under specific epithets, guardian of the threshold of the underworld and protector of the deceased, but sometimes she was the protective force the living world would need, such as for mothers about to give birth. These different roles can be seen in the various goddesses related to the sun that later had cults dedicated to them and mythologies written about them in other cultures.

Relationship of Hecate to the Hittite
Sun Goddess of Arinna

Some scholars believe that the goddess Hecate, who is thought to be originally from Anatolia, could have been a solar goddess before becoming the Greek queen of the underworld. This theory is based on the fact that Hittite prayers to the lady of Arinna, the Anatolian sun goddess, are similar to Greek prayers dedicated to Hecate. For example, the Anatolian sun goddess of the Earth is invoked to open the underworld by "old women" in a Hittite prayer, and Hesiod's prayer to Hecate follows the same pattern. This theory also assumes that Hecate was therefore a fusion of the sun goddess of Arinna and the Sumerian Ereshkigal and the later Greek goddess Artemis.

> Analyses of Hesiod's extended encomium of the goddess have provided plausible thematic reasons for her unusual prominence (Boedeker; Marquardt) but the prayer as a whole also shows remarkable parallels with second-millennium BCE Hittite royal prayers for the Sun-goddess of the sacred city Arinna, "torch of Hatti-land," one of the "Former Gods," found "in heaven, in the sea, or in the mountains," "whose divinity is honored among all the gods." She rules kings and queens, and makes king those on whom she looks with favor; she grants growth of grain, sheep, and cattle, and provides victory in war. Similarly, Hecate is a goddess who did not have to relinquish her powers on earth, sea, or in heaven when the Titans fell, but Zeus honored her above all. To whatever righteous person calls on her, Hecate can give prosperity and power: kings in the law-court, on the battlefield, shepherds, sailors, and athletes (Bachvarova 2010, 1).

Although I will discuss another possibility further on for the development of the goddess Hecate, it is important to note that Hecate is the daughter of Asteria, the goddess of the stars. Here is the hint that tells us that her association with the night sky is important. In prayers she may have been acting as a savior to her followers, a function that many solar deities shared. Although her origins are still mysterious and her functions evolved through time, Hecate made such an impression that she is still a main goddess in contemporary witchcraft. She passes through the underworld to embrace us, protect us, and lead us to rebirth.

SHAPASH

The less known goddess Shapash was revered as a sun deity within the Phoenician and Canaanite cultures. While her prominence diminished in later Ugaritic myths, compared to the era when solar cults held greater importance, she still played a significant role in certain narratives. As a sun goddess, Shapash aids the warrior goddess Anat in her quest to retrieve the body of the slain god Baal (a seasonal god) in an epic story called the Baal Cycle. This quest leads them to the entrance of the underworld, where Shapash's radiant light guides Anat to Baal (Smith 2014). This mythic tale possibly reflects the burial practices prevalent in these regions, suggesting a belief that the sun facilitated the journey of the deceased back home, symbolizing a form of rebirth. The concept of returning home signifies a renewal process wherein the departed souls ascend to the heavens to receive revitalizing energy. Rituals associated with ancestor worship often occurred during liminal periods, such as dawn or sunset, as it was believed in ancient times that the sun goddess guided souls to the underworld during sunset. The idea of departing with the setting sun holds a profound and beautiful symbolism, one that remains relevant in modern thought. Shapash was also a strong symbol of drought and death and her different roles in the Baal Cycle literature illustrate this very well (Wikander 2014, 2).

Because she was an all-seeing goddess, Shapash was a messenger of the cosmic god El, in late Ugaritic texts. She could have been the last remaining sun goddess of ancient Mesopotamia. The Canaanite people called her She-of-the-Corpse, referring to her important role of guarding the dead every night. Because her role was understood as crucial in the cult of the dead and ancestors, we even find traces of her in the Bible and the extra biblical texts written by ancient Hebrew people who were living in northern Syria.

ASHERAH

This next figure is still a mysterious and popular deity that challenges biblical scholars. In modern Jewish spirituality, many women try to reconnect with this ancestral goddess of the ancient land of the Israelite people. Asherah is mostly known for being the wife of god. Indeed, in the Ugaritic text she is the consort of El, the first important god of the ancient Hebrew people before Yahweh took his place. Therefore, Yahweh still had Asherah as a consort in some inscriptions from the biblical period (Stavrakopoulou 2017). The first mention of Asherah appears in Babylonian texts under the name Ashratum. She would have been an Amorite goddess brought to Mesopotamia by the Amorite ruling class during the second millennium. Her epithets included Lady of the Steppes and Wife of the Heavenly King. She was considered the consort of the time god Amurru, a divine representation of the Amorites. The kingdom of the Amorites spread from today's western Syria and Lebanon. The Amorites were a nomadic northwest Semitic-speaking people. The name Ashratum became associated to the Ugaritic Athirat, which was later translated as Asherah. This goddess was the deity of this nomadic tribe, which used to live in the mountains. She is a mother of the gods who was adapted to the different cultures that took her as their main deity: "Another title that is commonly ascribed to Athirat in the Ugaritic texts is *qnyt ilm*. This is most often translated as 'Creatress of the Gods,' or 'Progenitor of the Gods.' There is virtually no contention about this translation among scholars. Athirat is referenced in the texts as being the mother of the gods in many places" (Watkins 2007, 48).

Asherah is mostly related to trees and goats in iconography, if we can attest that these images are Asherah. Since Amurru was in fact a moon god, his consort was most likely a sun goddess or a particular aspect of the solar deity. With epithets such as "she who determines the day" (Watkins 2007, 47), she would determine fate among humans, as did most solar deities. In southern Arabia, Athirat (Asherah) is referred to as a sun goddess and was attributed with various epithets that likely referred to the solar disk as it moved in a seemingly straight line across the celestial vault, going from east to west. This imagery of the sun traversing the skies is also found in the biblical Psalms 19:6, where the sun is described as "running along a road."

Because Asherah was adopted elsewhere, in seaside towns, it seems she could have become a Lady of the Sea, making it difficult for many researchers to understand her (Watkins 2007, 48). It is best to think of her as a chief goddess with a long cultic story.

In Ugarit, her attendant is known as the sacred traveler (holy passer), tasked with journeying to Crete across the sea. He might have served as the ferryman for the sun goddess, who sails nightly across the ocean of the underworld. Indeed, the image of a boat in the iconography of the ancient Near East is often a symbol of the celestial realm of the underworld, as one traverses the sky by boat on the Milky Way river. The sun and the moon passing through the Milky Way at night and being reborn each morning symbolized the dance of Nut and the celestial moon and sun. Here again we find this reference regarding Athirat.

In this biblical allusion to the boat, we can see that the celestial realm was still important for the ancient Hebrews at the time of the writing of the Old Testament, and in some of its passages, we can still find traces of the cult of Asherah where she is mentioned in relation to trees about thirty times. As a powerful queen of heaven and Earth, linked to trees and sacred ponds, Asherah is, for me, the life-giving goddess linked to an ancient solar cult; she may even represent the day itself. As her epithet suggests, it could read Lady Day (Watkins 2007, 47). I would suggest that if Asherah represents the Milky Way or the underworld sun, her name may be better understood as Lady of Light. The temples dedicated to her and erected by King Solomon himself have been destroyed, as related in 2 Kings 23:7 of the Old Testament, where she was known to be worshipped alongside the moon, the sun, and other stars. Women dedicated to the cult of Asherah were weavers (Létourneau 2022). Asherah is responsible for the protection of women and their arts, represented by spinning and weaving and is most often worshipped as a statue of wood or a tree. She connects the heavens to the Earth. She is very much like the Slavic goddess Mokosh, who is responsible for weaving the destiny of humans. Mokosh is linked to the cult of sacred wells and is powerful in divination and healing. As such she is also associated with the Milky Way and the underworld sun and sometimes with the constellation Ursa Major. Just like Mokosh, the frequent mentions of the goddess Asherah in ancient biblical stories indicates references and connections to the celestial world, as the ancient Hebrews also used to worship the stars (Smith 2001).

Mother of the Gods and the Cult of Stones

The major divinities were of an astral nature, and their manifestations could be summoned into statues, trees, and stones. The ancient Mediterranean world rarely had anthropomorphic images of those deities. Although on seals and other art forms the imagery of the divine is identified either by human shapes or symbols taken from nature, or even animals, cult statues have never been found. Some say that it is because these statues were made of wood and so did not last, which was probably the case for most deities. The essence of specific woods was attributed to a god or goddess in particular.

The same applied to stones, but not just any stone or rock could be sacred; only those that were thought to have unique powers or were imbued with energy coming from the heavens. Such stones were also used to represent divinities because the stones were thought to be alive too. The most special stones were those that came directly from the gods' realm. Meteorites that had fallen from the sky were a very physical manifestation of the divine coming into this world. As such, they were especially venerated. The cultures of the Near East to the Roman Empire often associated them with the mother of the gods. According to ancient authors, ax-heads made of serpentine or jadeite were also seen as coming from the gods and therefore were used as amulets until medieval times (Faraone 2014). Three different types of stones were used as amulets, as exemplified here:

> *Cerauniae* are similar to axes (*similes . . . securibus*) and can be divided into two types by color and shape: the black and round ones called *baetyli*, which can be used aggressively to attack cities and navies; and the red and oblong ones called *cerauniae*. Sotacus does not mention any special powers for this second category, but he then goes on to remark that a third and rare type were sought out by *magi* in places that had been struck by lightning. (Faraone 2014, 2)

As is evident from these records, specific stones were believed to possess potent magical properties. Baetylus stones, for example, were used for divination and protection, and meteorite-based stones were particularly revered for their unique attributes. Meteorite stones, often shaped in ovoid forms, were said to have the ability to change colors and even communicate. Throughout the ancient world, devotees would perform circumambulation rituals around these stones, symbolizing the celestial journey of the meteorites in the sky. This reverence for stones stemmed from their perceived deity-like qualities. In ancient belief systems, stones not only harbored various powers but were also associated with gendered energies. Brightly colored stones were often viewed as masculine, while paler ones were considered feminine. Meteorites were seen as exceptions as they appeared uniformly dark—typically black and possessing a unique shine—and were believed to embody a feminine essence.*

ALLAT

In the pre-Islamic Arabian Peninsula, the main religious beliefs were tied to general Near Eastern beliefs, meaning that most deities in neighboring regions were similar to one another, varying only in their names. That was also true for the region of South Arabia, known today as Yemen. In these regions many goddesses were represented as stones. The most popular goddess, thought to be the mother of life, was known as Allat or Elat, linking her to the Elat from Syria. Elat in Syria was also known as Asherah, the consort of El. Some scholars believe that the pre-Islamic Allat could have been the same goddess as Asherah as a form of the sun goddess (Monaghan).

Allat was also worshipped with two other sisters, Al-Uzza and Al-Manat. They both represented, respectively, Venus and the moon, although later they were thought to be the daughters of the moon god. Al-Uzza was the morning aspect of Venus, and she had a masculine counterpart, Ashtart, who was the evening aspect of this planet. Al-Manat, associated with the moon, was

*See the *Picatrix*, a book of magic and astrology originally written in Arabic in the eleventh century.

the goddess of death. The ancient Nabateans and Arabs worshipped Allat in the shape of a four-sided stone. All three sisters were thought to be stones, as it was prevalent for the nomadic pre-Islamic and Hebrew desert tribes to worship deities in the form of stones. When the Arabian people founded Mecca, many deities were worshipped there. One stone stood out as having fallen from the sky, and it is speculated that this is the Black Stone currently housed in Kaaba or Bayt Allah (House of God) in Mecca (Farrington 1900). Today, the stone is located on the eastern side of the Kaaba, pointing toward the brightest star of the southern celestial hemisphere, the Canopus star. Although Islam has changed the beliefs of these people over the millennia, Muslims will gather at this very sacred site. Each pilgrim to Mecca must touch or kiss this sacred stone, dedicated to these sisters. In ancient beliefs, Allat was the judge of the afterlife, which, as we have seen, is the purview of solar and life goddesses. The Black Stone of Mecca, which holds powers, is still guarded by the walls of the Kaaba and still symbolizes the creation of life through the transformation of death. Allat is thought to have also been a warrior deity, which aligns with the protective aspect of an underworld deity. We sadly have little information about these ancient pre-Islamic goddesses. Some information contained in the Quran mentions that they were popular.

> In the fifth century, the Greek historian Herodotus mentions as the gods of the Arabs Orotalt and Alilat ('The Goddess'). In the Islamic Qur'an, al-Lat together with al-'Uzza and Manat are mentioned as daughters of Allah. They are also attested as divine names in earlier north Arabian inscriptions. There were also direct borrowings from Mesopotamia and Syria. The pantheon at Palmyra included Nergal (assimilated to the Greek Herakles), Nabû or Nebo (assimilated to Apollo), the Syrian goddess Atargatis, and possibly Astarte, that is Ištar (Inana), and Beltis (Bélet-ili). (Black & Green 1992, 35)

This is why the Prophet sought to dismantle these cults in the seventh century CE, favoring the worship of the lunar deity Allah (ibn-Al-Kalbi). A similar narrative unfolded among the ancient Hebrews centuries earlier, as they prohibited the veneration of trees and stones.

Finally, Allatu, also known as Alani, was the Hurrian version of Allat. Known as a death goddess, she was later introduced to the Hittite pantheon. She was equated with Sumerian Ereshkigal, the Sumerian queen of the underworld and sister to Inanna. She was often worshipped with Ishara, the equivalent to Ishtar, representing Venus. Allatu was one of the most important deities of the Hurrian world and as such received votives and offerings. She lives on the edge of the dark Earth, on an island with an entrance to the world of no return. Funerary customs related to her include songs and music. She is probably linked to the twilight western horizon.

Ancient Rome and the Sacred Ancilia

During the era of Numa, Rome's second king in the eighth century BCE, a legend recounts the descent of a diamond-shaped shield from the heavens. Simultaneously, Numa heard a divine voice proclaiming that this celestial omen signified Rome's destiny as the "mistress of the world, protected as long as the shield endured." Thus, Numa enshrined this sacred shield as a palladium, an object imbued with protective powers. Guided by the wise counsel of the goddess Egeria, Numa crafted eleven replicas of the shield to safeguard the original from theft. Egeria was revered as a spirit bestowing rituals and laws, her presence was marked by prophetic messages delivered through natural phenomena like lightning strikes—the same force that accompanied the ancile's celestial descent. In many aspects, Egeria bore similarities to the goddess Diana, embodying both mystical insight and protective guardianship.

The fact that this item fell from the sky and that it had an unusual shape led some to interpret it as a possible meteorite (McBeath and Gheorghe 2005, 136). Especially since the apparition of this object was preceded by thunder and loud noises and it was believed that it would cure disease. It could be an ancient legend reflecting the cult of meteorite stones. Other ancient texts tell the tales of strange objects falling from the sky that became important figures of specific cities. The roman goddess Magna Mater, for example, was also apparently worshipped as a stone. Various legends say that she fell from the sky and that she was not man-made. (McBeath and Gheorghe 2005, 138)

It appears that many goddesses are related to meteorites and other stones and that the energy emanating from these special geological items served the purpose of worshipping an entity that would protect and heal its people. I like to think that the creatrix was sometimes a visitor to her people.

SYMBOLIC MESSAGE

 *Rebirth*

The message that the creatrix sends to us is that life must die to be reborn. Just like winter brings death followed by the renewal of spring, life will return after death. The creatrix is a forceful reminder that time is eating us alive. The powerful infernal goddesses represent the many dangers of the winter season, but they also bring protection and luck into the next year when spring returns after the winter solstice. Observe the night sky during December and see how full of life and light the sky is, how powerful forces dance around us in this cycle of life. She rises again at the beginning of winter.

Let go of your current state and allow yourself to join the stars. Go deep inside to observe what you want to let go of and allow to die. Do not be afraid to go out in the dark at night to observe what you may be hiding during the day. It is not supposed to be easy; it will hurt and be hard. But this is the first step toward healing. If you can, try to spend one night under the night sky and ask for an answer to appear to you in a dream. This was an ancient method of divination in the ancient world. Think about the fact that the current world has created a big illusion. Break out of the mold and allow darkness to shine through. The night sky is, after all, very bright. Let go of narcissism. Let go of fear. Let go of unnecessary work. Let go of too much materialistic matter. Let go of relationships that bring no joy. Most of all, let go of the validation you seek through others. When you achieve all those steps, you will need no other validation than that of yourself. Your relationship with the goddesses will get stronger and better and your life freer.

HOW TO WORK WITH

The Creatrix

As we have explored in this first chapter, the energy of the great mothers is somewhat complex. However, it is not difficult to work with the energy of the creatrix. Because these creatrixes represented the light in the night sky itself, the essence of what brings life into the cosmos, it is no wonder that these figures were often consulted in matters concerning death and protection. The winter season is the best time to perform rituals and seek assistance from the powers of the celestial creatrix. Burning incense will set the mood, particularly incense made from tree resin and the heliotrope plant. A good way to commune with these entities is by spinning wool. The distaff and the spinning wheel are ancient symbols of the creatrix and have been used for generations as a potent magical tool for women. Through spinning, you can produce magical items, imbued with the energy of the dark goddess, that will bring you protection and luck. While you slowly spin the thread try to set intentions.

Slowly shed your ego, your fears. Let go of the control you want over your life, for time is not in your hands. Just try to feel peaceful and unified with the energies of the creatrix. You are in the hands of the weavers of life, the triple sisters, the great mothers, and only they will decide when your time is up. Let go of anything futile, anything that is not what you really want in life, for life is short. The mothers of the gods invite you to really live in the present, to live your life to the fullest, for they will call you soon to return to them. Have no fear, in the great darkness of the starry night you will be in the arms of the mothers. Let go of fear, so you can really live your life.

Visualize the luck, the outcome you would like to see in your life as you spin. Once you are done, you can either weave your yarn, if you know how, into cloth and make a garment that will be worn for luck or simply go to a little water pond that is sacred to you and leave the yarn on a tree as an offering to the creatrix. Traditionally, women would spin and weave together while singing a magical song. The celestial energies explored here are fond of singing, so do not hesitate to let your heart sing for the mothers of the cosmos. The Milky Way and the sun goddesses particularly like percussive sounds of all sorts, as such the ancient sistrum, a type of rattle, was used while dancing.

((O))

Potnia Theron on ancient Greek amphora, eighth century BCE
(National Archaeological Museum of Athens)

Photo by Zde

THE WARRIOR

Anat, Circe, Britomartis-Diktynna,
Aphaia, Athena

Celestial Bodies: Altair, sun, Aquila
Symbols: Eagle, hawk, bow and arrow, oak tree
Seasons: Summer and autumn
Symbolic Message: Seeking justice

*Hear me, Zeus's daughter, celebrated queen, Bromia and Titanis,
of a noble mien: in darts rejoicing, and on all to shine, torch-
bearing Goddess, Diktynna divine.*

ORPHIC HYMN XXXVI

There is much to be said about the protective nature of women. Although we live in a world that tries to tame the natural aggressiveness of the feminine, some goddesses were revered for this attribute. In fact, it was expected that male warriors received energy from the warrior goddesses. Men maintained personal relationships with goddesses, such as Odysseus had with Athena. Women must resist society's control over them and express their aggressive energy. Women are taught to be peaceful, harmless, and attractive, but there is a reason that the scariest divinity in India is the goddess Kali. She represents the epitome of divine feminine rage and the power of destruction and death. Women embracing their aggressive side does not mean they must be violent for no reason, but rather that they should be assertive and not allow the patriarchy to dominate them—and that goes for men too. The goddesses we explore in this chapter were often mostly adored by men and celebrated by women.

The ancient warrior goddess figure is an inspiration for me and has been following me since childhood. I was drawn to the warrior goddesses during my travels in Greece. I could feel a particular energy near the seas and the mountains, and I could sense these sacred places were watched over by ancient forces. Justice, retribution, death, and rebirth are among the meanings of this powerful solar symbol, a testimony of ancient forces of eternal youth. In this chapter, I explore the warrior goddesses with strong symbolic links to the eagle and birds of prey.

The Sacred Triangle

When I arrived at the Temple of Aphaia on the island of Aegina in June 2021, I learned that this temple formed a sacred triangle with two other temples. The ancient Greek temples, monuments, and sanctuaries were meticulously designed with precise symmetry. These structures, ranging from altar pieces to entire cities, followed perfect geometric patterns and mathematical principles. This dedication to symmetry was believed to mirror the celestial harmony of the cosmos and the fundamental laws of the universe.

Modern scholars have extensively studied notable examples of this architectural symmetry, such as the isosceles triangle formed by the Temple of Poseidon at Cape Sounion, the Temple of Aphaia on Aegina Island, and the Temple of Hephaestus in Thission, Athens. Another triangle formed by the Temple of Apollo at Delphi, the Parthenon in Athens, and the Temple of Aphaia at Aegina has also been analyzed. I personally visited the triangle formed by the three temples of Aphaia, Sounio, and Hephaestus, and there is indeed a palpable sense of magical energy emanating from these sacred sites. It has been proposed that these triangular formations reflect celestial phenomena observed in the night sky, which is a plausible theory. I even speculated that it might be connected to the Summer Triangle, a prominent triangle in the northern celestial hemisphere defined by the stars Altair, Deneb, and Vega.

When I looked at the sky during the night, I noticed, because it was summer, that the Eagle constellation was overhead. I had noticed in previous research that the hawk or eagle was often associated with goddess figures, but I did not understand why. I started to think that maybe the warrior figures were symbols of the Eagle star. As we explore in this chapter, the eagle is also a figure of the deceased world and caring for the dead.

Eagle Lore in the Ancient Worldview

In Mesopotamia, the constellation Aquila was known as a symbol of the eagle. It may have originated from the Anzubird, a powerful half-lion half-bird creature who, since the fourth millennium BCE, brought retribution to evildoers. The eagle would snatch the souls of people who did not deserve to return to the realm of the ancestors, and they would disappear below the horizon. The eagle as a symbol of justice resonates very much with the goddesses I explore in this chapter. In ancient Greece we find that eagle symbolism is also associated with Nemesis, a winged goddess who personified justice and retribution, punishing, in particular, those who commit the sin of hubris.

There has been a suggestion from author Gavin White that the Mesopotamian eagle could also be a symbol of birth, as he sees that the eagle also brings children's souls to Earth. This is interesting because the "eagle stone," also known as Aetite, was understood to be a magical stone for birthing mothers, as seen in the *Picatrix*. He suggests that "as a symbol, the eagle transports souls to and from the ancestral realm continuum, which is simultaneously the destination of the dead and the well-spring of new life" (White 2014, 128).

The dual aspect of divine justice and bringer of life, as depicted by the eagle, fits perfectly with the figure of the violent warrior goddess.

ANAT

In ancient Mesopotamian literature, Anat is not very prevalent, and for a long time, many forgot this wonderful goddess, but her name is still sacred for many Syro-Palestinian communities. Anat was better known throughout the Mediterranean as an important warrior goddess. She is known in the Ugaritic literature from the Bronze Age as a ferocious maiden warrior, protecting her brother Baal (KTU, 26–39).* Although not proven, according to some, an etymological root suggestion for the name Anat is the Arabic word *anwat*, which means "force, violence" (Cornelius 2008, 92). Her iconography frequently presents her with a hammer in a striking pose—and later on, with a bow and arrow. She was seen as an eternal adolescent figure, explaining why she was understood as a maiden. The armed and ferocious Anat was a strong symbol of royalty and protection, an inspiration to young women.

In Ugaritic poetry, Anat violently slays the hero Aqhat to gain the bow and arrows that belonged to her (KTU 1.18). It is said that she tried to seduce Aqhat to retrieve them, but he refused her. She then tricked him into attending a hunting party and then transformed herself into a hawk and killed him. What we learn from that legend is that the sacred bow was intended for the goddess but was given to the mortal instead, which caused Anat to act violently—much like the goddess Inanna. Because she killed the hero, an agricultural fertility god, a famine came over the land. How the story concludes is not known because the text is missing. The common understanding of this myth is that it tries to explain why drought occurs during summer, making it more difficult to produce food.

It is not unusual that Anat is linked with the hawk and drought. Primarily because in the ancient Near East, including Egypt, the hawk (or eagle) is associated with the sun (Marinatos 2000, 35). This association endured later in Greece as well. The sun was understood as something sacred but also cruel, given that these regions could suffer from too much

---

*KTU or Keilalphabetische Texte aus Ugarit is the standard reference for the cuneifrom texts from Ugarit.

sunshine, causing the crops to die. But it would be too simple to presume that the story of Anat is only a symbol of drought: her story would be more complex than that.

Another epic poem from Ugarit is called the Epic of Baal. The god Baal, whose name means "lord," was understood as a fertility figure, lord of rain and dew, a general Earth god found in many Near Eastern cultures. Anat is Baal's sister, which makes sense—to have sun and rain as brother and sister. But was Anat only a sun goddess? Maybe not. In the epic, Anat resurrects Baal when he dies. She not only protects him in all his adventures, but she also brings him back to life. That's quite an important role! We know that a very ancient mythological motif is that the sun dies at the summer solstice to be reborn at the winter solstice. Celebrations were organized around the sudden lessening of sunlight toward the end of the year and the return of light near the end of winter. Another general conception was that the world is conceived in spring, gestates through summer and autumn, and is born at the winter solstice in December, a narrative found in almost every ancient culture and even the modern one.

What is striking, though, is the imagery of the hawk and the bow. We know that, just like the Mesopotamians, the Canaanites and the ancient Hebrews did have a religion centered around astral powers (Smith 2001). Almost all of their literature is referenced in a way that can be understood as celestial stories of the sky (Smith 2001). For example, the Babylonians associated the Aquila constellation, which appears clearly in the northern sky, with the eagle, as did the Romans—the name Aquila is Latin for "eagle." The Greeks understood Aquila to be Zeus's falcon, who transported his thunderbolts. According to a researcher, the Eagle constellation was once seen by the Babylonians as transporting a dead man with a bow and arrow; some think that it could be Sagittarius (Krüger 2012). The Sagittarius constellation is indeed very close to the Eagle.

It is hard to not see here the story of Anat and the hero Aqhat, as Anat in the guise of a hawk transported the dead body of the hero Aqhat. But what about the resurrection of Baal? It is said that the Aquila constellation is mainly visible in the night sky from July to October in the northern celestial hemisphere, being its brightest during autumn, and then reappears very clearly at dusk during the winter solstice. Maybe this feature made the ancients think that when the goddess comes back, the sun comes back too. Aquila, the Eagle star, is part of three important stellar objects that make up the sacred triangle, which was discussed at the beginning of this chapter.

If we view Anat as the embodiment of the Eagle constellation in connection to the sun, what insights does her cult provide? Her worship spans from the late third millennium to the fourth century BCE, with her prominence growing notably in the Late Bronze Age, particularly during the thirteenth century BCE when the Egyptians incorporated her into their beliefs, especially during the Ramesside era. She had dedicated temples in Egypt, such as in Tanis and Hibis, where she was associated with military might and served as the favored and patron goddess of Ramses II, symbolized by her donning of the royal crown (*atef*). This imagery signifies her role as both protector of kings and as a legitimizing force for pharaonic power (Stuckey 2003). This aligns with the traditional role of many goddesses in ancient cultures, where they bestowed divine authority upon kings. In iconography depicting a goddess nursing an infant, the child typically symbolizes a young god or king, signifying their divine embodiment and the goddess as their symbolic mother, thus granting the king the right to rule as a divine being. This concept mirrors personal transformation through initiation, where dedicating oneself to the path of the goddess facilitates spiritual ascent and empowerment.

In Palestine, under Egyptian rule, Anat had temples in the city of Beisan, now called Beth-shean, and festivals were given in her honour at Gaza. The old city is located on a mound between the Jordan River and the Jezreel Valley and is bounded by the Mount Gilboa mountain range on the southwest. According to the Ugarit texts, Anat made her home on Mount Inbb, which has never been located. She may have had altars dedicated to her in the caverns located in the mountains near Beth-shean, as was a common practice in the Bronze Age. Many goddesses were worshipped on mountaintops, altars being found in caverns, because they were the highest point to the sky.

The following hymn dedicated to Anat was found in the Ugaritic texts. The text is fragmented but seems to be an invocation hymn. We learn that her home is located high up and that eagles are kin to her. The hymn mentions unidentified little creatures, which she chases. It seems that it is an invocation hymn against poisonous serpents' bites.

> *Go and fly to your Eagle race*
> *And rest on your mountain of the Ebbn*
> *Come to your mountain that I know*
> *Come to us, come to your home in the skies**

Sadly, only a portion of the section following this hymn remains, but it states that the stars would fall and the hunchbacks would flee from the cavern where her altar lies. Hunchbacks meant bad luck in ancient Mesopotamia, so it probably meant that her return would purify the place from evil sources. To invoke her for protection against evil is totally in tune with her task of protecting those who work with her. As names were sources of power in ancient times, to know the name of her house would ensure that you invoked the right energy. In this case, the eagle goddess from Ebbn, known as Anat.

On a stela in Egypt is the image of a nude goddess holding lotus flowers and flanked by lions. She has a solar crown on her head and is standing between the gods Min and Reshep. This stela is known as "Stele of the scribe Ramose dedicated to goddess Quetesh" (twelfth to thirteenth century BCE). This image, popular in the Levant, continues to intrigue researchers. Scholars have identified the goddess as Qetesh, Quedeshet, or even Qdushu; however, the writings on the stone mention two other names in additon to Qetesh: Anat and Astarte.

Qetesh is not well known and information about her is scarce; only in recent years have scholars differentiated her from Astarte. It has been

---

*Author's translation from the French in Cazelles, "L'Hymne Ugaritique a Anat," 52.

suggested that the Egyptians may have fused those three goddesses into one in the form of Qetesh. Because the goddesses' roles both overlapped and complemented one another, it is not impossible that Qetesh represents the almighty power of all three goddesses. In my opinion, it is plausible because this image is found on many amulets, and I have concluded that these amulets represent powerful protective magic. Qetesh is called Mistress of the Stars and Lady of the Stars of Heaven (Cornelius 2008, 76). These epithets represent the astral aspect of the goddess and her sovereignty over potent magic. Indeed, Anat and her sister Astarte were both also very potent against poison. We can assume that the Eagle or Aquila constellation related to the sky goddess figures of Anat and possibly Qetesh was a source of power and magic for sorceresses and priestesses.

We have seen that the hawk figure was linked to protective and apotropaic powers of the goddess exalted from the constellation. But we will now observe how this figure continued to travel with the Phoenicians to Greek, Cretan, and Anatolian territories. Anat is thought to have been the Queen of Heaven mentioned in the Bible; it seems she was sometimes associated with this title, although her function and symbolism is more related to her ability to protect. What is interesting about these goddesses with solar-eagle symbolism is that their relationship to the astral world is less direct than other goddesses.

CIRCE

Circe is known from the *Iliad* written by Homer, a literary piece that scholars agree was written during the Greek Archaic period (around eighth and ninth century BCE). In the story the sorceress Circe transforms Odysseus's companions into animals. To save them, Odysseus must agree to be Circe's lover, but as we will see, she never meant to make that request in the first place. Although he agrees to lie with her, there are no details about the rest of their night together. We know that an entire year passed by in what seems to be just one night for them. The symbolic play here is quite interesting. Circe is a mistress of animals, just like other goddesses, but she hides something else. In her name lies the answer to who she is. Indeed, Circe in Greek is Kirke, which means "hawk," and she is the daughter of the sun (Marinatos 2000, 35).

When Odysseus's men hear Circe sing and see her weaving, they go to her lair. It is no surprise to find that she lives deep in the forest surrounded by wolves and bears. That certainly means that she lives on a mountain. Although she is a dangerous force for men, as she transforms all of them into animals, she does not use her sexuality to lure them. Hermes warns Odysseus that Circe will enchant him by feeding him a poisonous plant, which will transform him into a beast, and suggests that, to stop her, Odysseus will have to lie in bed with her. Although Circe seems like she is the seductress, it looks more like she has to give her sexual power to the hero to save herself but also to help him:

> There I stood, at the gate of the goddess of the lovely tresses, and I called to her and she heard my voice. She came out straight away to open the shining doors, and invited me to enter. I did so, with a troubled heart. Once inside she brought me a beautiful silver-embossed chair, richly made, and with a stool for my feet. Then she mixed me a drink in a golden cup, and with evil intent added her drugs. When she gave it me, and I drank it down, though without feeling its enchantment, she struck at me with her wand, and cried: "Off to your sty now, and lie there with your friends." At this, I drew my sharp sword and rushed at her, as if I meant to kill her, but with a cry she slipped beneath the blade to clasp my knees, and weeping spoke to me with winged words: "What man are you, and where are you from? What city is yours? And who are your parents?*

As discussed previously, sexuality in the ancient world was often linked to a relationship of power. Sexual symbolism characterizes the power that is taken away or given to some worthy characters. The powerful Circe hence is forced to give her blessings to the hero Odysseus so that

---

*Homer: *The Odyssey*, Book X: 302–47, "Odysseus Tells His Tale: Encountering Circe," Poetry in Translation website.

he may be successful in his quest. In the story she helps him with a type of divination that was widely used by women: necromancy, which was used to communicate with the dead and spirits to receive important information. Circe tells Odysseus how to go to the underworld and therefore how to communicate with the dead. In the ancient world this was a skill that most witches would have and that would define them as such.

If we look outside the poem, we can also find Circe in the ancient lore of the Mediterranean. There is in Italy Mount Circeo, which is believed to have been the mythical island of Circe, especially as it has been translated as the mountain of the hawk. But no traces of cult activity have been found there. We, nonetheless, know humans did live in those caves in Neanderthal times. The mystical island of Aeaea, which is associated with Circe, is also thought to be either the Greek Paxos island or Croatian Lošinj, or even Cyprus. Aeaea, which means "eagle," could also have been an epithet of the goddess. As such, it is also believed that she lives with her brother Aeetes, also a child of the sun, like Circe. He is also the king of the kingdom of the Colchis, located near the Black Sea. Again, here we have references to eagles and the sun. Circe was especially connected to magical plants and medicinal herbs (Rhodius, bk. 4, 662 ff). In Roman times, she became the daughter of Hecate in the stories and myths, where she invoked the night sky and stars (Flaccus, bk. 7, 210 ff). Circe is therefore an ancient mistress of animals and a nature protector, represented as a powerful solar figure.

Now let's have a look on other islands and see if we still find hawk-eagle symbolism.

BRITOMARTIS-DIKTYNNA

During the Bronze Age, the Minoan people were living on the island of Crete. They are known today because of the famous palace of Knossos and the legendary King Minos and his labyrinth. There is no doubt that the cultural influence of the Minoans spread far and wide. During early phases of their culture, they were known to have cultic worship sites on mountain peaks, called the Minoan peak sanctuaries. We know that goddesses were revered on mountaintops. Because the Minoans' alphabet has not been completely deciphered, we do not know all the names of their deities. But after the Late Bronze Age collapse, the people who stayed on the island of Crete did have names from memories of the Minoans.

The Minoan religion was deeply rooted in animism and a profound connection with nature. Their intricate iconography revealed reverence for all living creatures and a close bond with elements like trees, stars, and bees. Trees held particular significance in ancient religions, especially in the Eastern Mediterranean, serving as altars and symbols of royalty.

A notable study conducted in 1894 by Jean N. Svoronos examined coins from Crete, shedding light on the iconography of a significant goddess in Minoan culture. These fifth-century BCE coins depict a goddess seated atop a tree resembling an oak, portrayed in a regal manner with a hawk by her side and a royal scepter in hand. This goddess, identified as Britomartis, is associated with astronomical symbolism representing the movements of the sun and moon (Svoronos 1894). It's worth noting that the hawk symbolizes the sun's power, while Britomartis's connection to Artemis adds a lunar aspect, highlighting the fusion of both solar and lunar energies.

The cult of Britomartis traveled from Phoenicia to Crete. She had a temple on Mount Tytyros near the ancient city of Kydonia, now modern Chania. Kydonia was a Minoan city that flourished from 1700 to 1200 BCE and was known for commercial ties with the island of Aegina. After the Minoan culture vanished, it was taken over by the Doric people and eventually by colonizers from Aegina.

Scholars translate the name Britomartis as "good maiden," "sweet maiden," or "blessed maiden." Just like Anat and many warrior goddesses, she was considered a goddess of mountain and nature, an eternal maiden not interested in the company of men. She most likely bore two names on Aegina, Britomartis and Diktynna—as the ancient Greek historians Diodorus, Pausanias, and Callimachus have mentioned. She was known as Diktynna only in Kydonia, as it refers to the mountain where she was worshipped. This epithet links her to the place where she lived, but does not indicate what her role was. In some later myths she is described as being a huntress who spends all of her time with the goddess Diana. She was sometimes equated with Artemis, as people considered her a protector of animals and women. Although her cult is very old, the myths about Britomartis came to us only in later times through Greek historians, who tried to explain how she came to be known in some areas.

Her relationship with mountains and with the solar hawk can therefore lead us to believe that she may be related to another form of the Anat figure. According the Greek grammarian Antoninus Liberalis (ca. 100–300 CE), in his *Metamorphoses* (poem 40), Britomartis came from the Levant. She probably is the mistress of animals, a goddess role that we find everywhere in the Near East, and she was important in relation to divination and protection. For certain, she was the epitome of a nature goddess. We can find accounts that Britomartis was also worshipped in Kefalonia, an island in the Ionian sea. There she may have been called Laphria. We know of a festival called the same name in honor of Artemis, which was held in the city of Patras overlooking the Gulf of Patras. According to Nilsson (1950), there is little doubt that the Britomartis figure is considered a mistress of animals.

As we have explored, the hunter goddess is always a protective figure, and the celebration of this ancient goddess, who became mostly known as Diktynna during the Hellenistic period, is also a testimony that people relied on protection from this goddess. Britomartis-Diktynna is a goddess of light, of the reborn sun.

APHAIA

In poem 40 of his *Metamorphoses*, Antoninus Liberalis notes: "The Aiginetans consecrated the place in which Britomartis disappeared and named her Aphaia and accomplished sacrifices as to a goddess." When I heard that the Temple of Aphaia was still standing almost intact on the island of Aegina, I had to go see it. Located on the top of a mountain, the views of the sea were spectacular, and I could feel that she was the center of a very profound and nature-based cult. On my visit, the sky was clear, and so the starry sky at night must have been magical.

We already mentioned that the Aegina people were known to the Kydonians and they were very much aware of their goddess. Some say that the people of Aegina had a vision of Diktynna and called her the Invisible One, known as Aphaia. It is a peculiar name, and I did try to find the meaning, but without much luck. Is the invisible one a stellar object? In much later Greek myths, it is said that Britomartis tried to escape the nonconsensual embrace from Minos on the island of Crete. She would hide herself in oak foliage on top of her mountain to make sure he didn't see her. When Minos eventually found her, she jumped into the sea, and fishermen from Aegina caught her in their nets. This story is a late invention and even in Greek times, some doubts have been cast on its origin. This story would have been made up to explain how Britomartis came to Aegina. It is noteworthy to mention that Aphaia is the only goddess bearing this name in all of Greece, and she is exclusively worshipped there.

Another interesting myth suggests that the island of Aegina was named after a nymph of the same name. Zeus took on the appearance of an eagle and carried the nymph to to the island Oenone. She gave birth to the mythical king of Aegina called Aecus. Again, our goddess is linked with the symbol of the hawk. Because this myth was created later in history, we can see the shift in the narrative. The goddess was once the hawk or eagle, associated with the solar and royal power. This bird would chase unworthy men and protect those in need. Eventually, Zeus became this powerful figure, and he took over all the symbolism to assimilate the goddesses, hence why so many rape stories are involved with him. Some say that Aphaia is maybe an epithet of Aegina itself.

There were other gods and goddesses on the island of Aegina although the highest and biggest temple was the one for Aphaia. The Greek Pausanias tells us that:

Of the gods, the Aeginetans worship most Hecate, in whose honor every year they celebrate mystic rites which, they say, Orpheus the Thracian established among them. Within the enclosure is a temple; its wooden image is the work of Myron, and it has one face and one body. It was Alcamenes, in my opinion, who first made three images of Hecate attached to one another, a figure called by the Athenians Epipurgidia (on the Tower); it stands beside the temple of the Wingless Victory. (Pausanias, bk. 2, 30.3)

This information from Pausanias is interesting because the Thracians were from the Balkans and Asia Minor, which comprises most of Turkey today. There is once again a mention of the goddess cult coming from the East. We have seen in the first chapter how the underworld solar symbol is also linked to Hecate. Even more interesting is how the mysteries of Hecate were celebrated on the island, probably intertwined with the mystery cult of Aphaia, which had started long before. Indeed, underneath the Temple of Aphaia you can find the entrance to a cavern, a sacred entrance to the underworld. In this cavern were found terracotta figures from the Myceanean and Minoan periods, further strengthening the hypothesis that Aegina was linked to the ancient Minoan culture starting in the fourteenth century BCE. These are known as votive offerings, in the shape of female with arms standing toward the sky. Some have bird-like facial features, which we can find on other islands in the Mediterranean.

Pausanias even tells us that the rites on Aegina were similar to those happening at Eleusis, saying that the sacrifices to the deities were about the same: "I saw the images, and sacrificed to them in the same way as it is customary to sacrifice at Eleusis" (Pausanias, bk. 2, 30.4). That means that the cults on Aegina are linked to death and rebirth, which is appropriate for a solar or chthonic figure, as we have observed in the first chapter.

On the mountain where the temple stands today, the land has been occupied since the fourth millennium. Before the Doric period, a very ancient temple dedicated to a goddess on Aegina was built on top of the mountain overseeing the Saronic Gulf. Some think it was the cult of the goddess Eugonia, a name that means "well-born." Later, this goddess came to be known as Aphaia, the Cretan goddess Britomartis, according to the locals of Aegina. This marvel of the ancient world still stands today amid a pine forest. Its architecture inspired the other Doric buildings including the Parthenon. A Doric temple was later built at the site of this sanctuary.

Adherents to the cult of Aphaia made a long pilgrimage from the village by the seaside to the temple on top of the mountain. No burials were found near the temple, indicating that it was used for rituals only. Some suggest that the structure was similar to temples dedicated to Artemis during the late Archaic period. Indeed, the original image of Aphaia is similar to that of Artemis Orthia, both depicted with wings. During the Classical era, when Athens became dominant, Aphaia became associated with Athena: therefore sculptures of heroes narrating the Trojan War were found on pediments with Athena standing in the middle of the scenes. The Athena association fits with the period that the Athenians took over Aegina. The temple was closed during the pagan persecution of the late Roman Empire.

Just like some features of Artemis, in which they were absorbed, Aphaia-Britomartis are known to be protectors of women in labor and childbirth, which is appropriate with the eagle and hawk symbolism, although their first and foremost function is the warrior-like protection of their peoples and of all sacred life. Today this goddess still strikes the imagination. The Minoan culture and its very ancient deities still have many secrets to share for the next generations. Their energy is still very inspiring to the sacred land of Greece, and hopefully their stories will continue to be shared.

ATHENA

Athena is a wonderful and complex goddess, and she fits our bird-maiden-warrior symbolism as well. Many scholars agree that Athena got her name from the city of Athens, therefore, she bears other names in other regions. Gods and goddesses were often named after the cities they were looking after, at least in Greece. Athena is linked mostly to crafting and wisdom. She is Odysseus's patroness and muse, and her wise counsel is apparent in the Homeric *Iliad*. Her figure is complex to analyze because she became a symbol of Athens itself and therefore encompasses the qualities of almost all the other goddesses at a certain point, mostly from the Classical era. She may have originated from the Bronze Age Mycenaeans' goddess Potnia Theron, shown as a warrior and sometimes a mistress of animals. With time, though, Athena became a figure of the *polis*—the city and civilized world. If she ever was the mistress of animals, she lost that role when her cult was transferred to the city. It is also worth mentioning that the mistress of animals figure became later associated with Artemis. She became the patron of forests and animals in Greece, and laws against deforestation have been made in her honor.

There is a distinction between the Mistress of Animals figure in Archaic Greece and those in the Minoan and Levantine regions. Rather than protecting animals, the figure appears to exert control over them, suggesting a symbol of civilization's dominance over nature. This transformation into Athena is conceivable if viewed through this lens. Some scholars propose her initial association with a bird of prey before adopting the owl as her symbol. The owl presents an intriguing aspect as it traditionally symbolizes the underworld, night, spirits, and communication with the deceased, yet it remains a bird of prey. This association brings to mind the ancient cults of Athena, possibly linked to the dead and ancestors, providing a potential explanation for her displacement of Aphaia.

Athena is commonly portrayed wearing the gorgoneion amulet, characterized by a demon face known in Greece as Gorgon, but potentially originating from a Near Eastern protective demon akin to Humbaba and Bes (Marinatos 2000). These amulets served to ward off malevolent spirits and misfortune, underscoring Athena's role as a protector and akin to Anat, a goddess who repels malevolent forces. An inscription from Phoenicia hints at Anat being identified with Athena, emphasizing their connection and Anat's significance. Consequently, it appears that Athena initially functioned as a warrior goddess but gradually assimilated additional roles over time. This evolution aligns with the Athenians' expansion in Greece, as Athena became their guardian deity. Prior to the construction of her temple on the Acropolis of Athens, she possessed a celestial aspect and was venerated in funerary practices. Notably, on the Acropolis, there is also a sanctuary dedicated to the nymph Pandrosos and her two siblings.

Pandrosos, meaning "all dew," was a goddess who served Athena. Her name, related to the morning dew, suggests that dew goddesses like Pandrosos are associated with the dawn. Dew was considered a blessing from the sky and was important for flowers and crops. In folkloric magic it is believed that washing your face with dew on the morning of Easter can give youth and beauty. Pandrosos and Athena, who are still found on the Acropolis, received cults dedicated to them by Athenian women. Young girls participated in a chthonic cult during the night, a rite of passage of symbolic death of their maiden state to become adolescent: "There was an underground enclosure under the Akropolis that was the setting for a nocturnal ritual during the annual summer ceremony, and it was to this enclosure the two young Arrephoroi went during the festival dedicated to Athena" (Håland 2012, 261).

Legend has it that Athena's original temple housed a statue believed to have fallen from the heavens, as described: "Her renowned statue, crafted from olive wood, resided in her 'old temple' (later in the Erechtheum); some claimed it descended from the sky" (Papachatzis 1989, 177). When I explored the sanctuary on the Acropolis, I encountered a magnificent olive tree, evoking a sense of an earlier cult devoted to an ancient goddess of death and rebirth, eventually assimilated by Athena.

Athena, with her regenerative abilities, symbolizes an ancient deity embodying nature and the hawk, eventually assimilated into human civilization. It is time to revive this forgotten aspect of the divine feminine, reminding us that eternal youth's energy is a force for life's enhancement. Ancient maidens and female warriors were protectors of nature and custodians of nocturnal magic, embodying a fierce and natural guardianship.

SYMBOLIC MESSAGE

✆ *Seeking Justice* ✆

The message of the maiden warrior is one of justice and of retribution to those who do not respect the sacredness of the Earth. She is a force that calls those who can hear the goddess message to fight for what is right. Her magical powers reside in the strength that can be brought forth to help us, and she can be used to punish others. Her work is most potent when relating to helping women, animals, and the environment. She asks that every one of us act, or else retribution will come. To gain knowledge of power in yourself to work with this potent energy, you will have to choose a battle you want to fight for. IF you do your best to keep fighting for it, the maiden warrior will guide you.

HOW TO WORK WITH

The Warrior

As you are now familiar with death and have worked on shedding the unnecessary burden from your life, you are now ready to take action and power into your hands. The best way to work with this star of destiny is to do volunteer work during the summer and autumn. As the oak and olive trees are associated with this energy, you can also make yourself an amulet made of oak or olive wood to protect yourself. I recommend working at night under the Altair and Sagittarius constellations and meditating about your strengths and values. Burning myrrh and frankincense is preferable.

Close your eyes and bathe under the starry night. I want you to think about what you offer to the world, what change are you able to make in your everyday life? What are your gifts and strengths and how do they better your life? Do you let others destroy everything around you or do you stand up? I want you to stand up. I want you to fight and not be afraid to denounce those who cause unjust violence and suffering. Everyone, including yourself, can make a difference, and by your service to the community, your serve the goddesses. Protect the environment, protect lives, and make the world a better place for future generations and the common good. This is the legacy of the maiden warrior: do not forget her ancient powers. This celestial energy likes martial arts and the practice of archery. If that is something you can do, this is a good way to honor this goddess.

《O》

Bust of Isis-Sothis-Demeter, white marble, Roman artwork, second part of Hadrian's reign, ca. 131–138 CE (from the gymnasium in the Villa Adriana, near Tivoli, 1736)

THE HEALER

Gula-Bau, Ataegina, Hecate,
Goddess of the Night, Artemis-Diana

Celestial Bodies: Vega, Sirius, Lyra, Ursa Major
Symbols: Dog, goat, bear
Seasons: Summer and winter solstices
Symbolic Message: Facing vulnerability

Both the keys to the gates of the Underworld as well as the guarantee of resurrection were in the hands of the Goddess. The initiation itself was like a voluntary death and a gracious salvation.

APULEIUS ON HIS INITIATION INTO
THE MYSTERIES OF ISIS, CA. 200 CE
(METAMORPHOSIS XI, 2)

Since the beginning of time, women have been seen as great healers but not as official doctors. Midwives were known for their herbal medicine and skills in surgery. But the healing midwife eventually became the figure of the witch. In this chapter, we encounter the great figures of healing magic and the symbols of today's witchcraft. I particularly love that the oldest figure of divine magic is linked to the symbol of the goat, which is still an animal related to witchcraft. In this chapter I present star energies that are often linked to the night. Mostly because, yes, the rituals were held at night but also because they are today known as dark goddesses, symbols of moon magic. The reason for this is that these goddesses had an important link with the dead and communicated with them. They were held sacred and important for the prevention of death by their healing powers, but they were also used as weapons against enemies. In this chapter we encounter the great Mesopotamian goddess Gula and the dark Hittite goddess of the night. I then present the importance of Sirius and the possible origins of the goddess Hecate and the healing legacy of Artemis and Diana.

Goat Lore in the Ancient Near East

Goddesses are almost always associated with goats. The goat was identified with women in ancient Near Eastern literature. For many years researchers thought it was because the goat was a source of food and an animal easily found everywhere, which is true—the goat was one of the first animals to be domesticated and was a source of milk for babies in prehistoric times.

The goat is a resilient animal and has been a powerful symbol, imbued with magical properties and used in religious rituals, since the dawn of times. The goat was considered wise, and in ancient Mesopotamia, its entrails were used for divination, called haruspicy. Sometimes a goat was enlisted for divination rituals but without using parts of the dead animal. In exorcism rituals, a goat was almost always present, either a live one or the figurine of a goat. The goat performed the function of a scapegoat: the demonic forces possessing the sick person were transferred to the goat. It was believed that if someone was possessed by a demon, that this demonic force was the source of illness. Although there are many types of demons, exorcist incantations commonly dealt with illness as the consequence of demonic possession.

> May he be radiant like a star, may the protective spirit of health
> approach with a healthy goat
> May the patient be wiped clean like copper, may the evil Utukku-
> demon . . . [missing part]
> May the personal god of that person be present at his head
> And may they bind the goat to the head of the distraught patient

Be that man be entrusted into the benevolent hands of his
    personal god
Through an offering to obtain me (radiance), make the healthy
    goat into a scapegoat*

In the exorcism ritual, the goat would be attached to the head of the sick man. Once the exorcist had lured the demon into the goat, the man would be free from illness, and the goat—either figurine or live animal—would be buried. This ritual was called the "scapegoat."

It is interesting to note as well the vocabulary linked to the stars. The radiance of the stars was a symbol of health and vitality and the healing spirits coming from there would bring health from this realm. Drinking vessels and libation jars were often depicted with goats as well, leading to the idea that their powers of cunning, wisdom, and vitality would then be transferred to the person who drank from those vessels (Breniquet 2002, 145–68). Even today, the goat continues to be associated with witches and magic, as it has been for millennia.

GULA-BAU

The ancient healing goddesses Bau and Gula were very important deities in the Western Asiatic world. These divine feminine figures were thought to be linked to specific stars and constellations. Hence, here we explore how the constellation Lyra, called the goat star in ancient Mesopotamia, is related to the great goddess of medicine Gula-Bau. She was invoked for astral irradiation and is possibly at the origins of lore of underworld goddesses related to healing and protection prevalent in the Mediterranean world.

The ancient Babylonians called the brightest star in the Lyra constellation the goat star—what we now call Vega. Vega was the pole star in 12,000 BCE, so it might have still been symbolically relevant when civilizations started to write or at least all the lore associated to this very important star survived through oral tradition. This star was so important that there is

---

*This incantation comes from a compendium of Mesopotamian exorcistic incantations called Udug-hul.

an extended medical corpus associated with it; therefore, the she-goat was understood as a healing deity and protector of the land of the deceased.

As early as the end of the third millennium, the Lyra constellation was called Mul-uz. At first, this name is not linked to a deity's name, but it could have been recognized as a goat figure first, before being connected to a particular goddess (Kurtik, 341–42). Although Mul-uz could also have eventually been an epithet of Inanna. It has been suggested that the Lyra constellation could have been linked to the heliacal rising of the Capricorn constellation, as this constellation appears in the northern celestial hemisphere in December. Goat lore all around the northern world is very prevalent in December. But since the star Vega is most visible during summer, although never setting in Europe, there is not enough evidence to attest this could be the reason Vega was once called the goat star. My suggestion is that the goat star was at first seen as a goddess of rebirth and healing and eventually this star got associated with the names of Bau-Gula and others.

We find other goddesses associated with rebirth and the goat figure such as possibly the goddess Asherah. I think that in the Mesopotamian world, this goddess was lost to Gula, but we can still find her in other territories such as the Levant and even in the Iberian Peninsula. As a goddess of life, the she-goat star is also an underworld mistress, giving rebirth to those who serve her. The mix of this deity with Gula will give us the origins, I think, of the very popular Hecate, as I explain further on. Indeed, the healing goddess was still present in the Greek magical texts centuries later. Hecate is associated in these magical texts as a goat and the goddess of the underworld Ereshkigal. This figure did endure through times, although her name changed and got mixed up with other goddesses. As noted earlier, this conflation was very common in the ancient world, which makes the study of goddesses and their origins very complicated. Gula, also called Bau or Baba in the Mesopotamian lore, was a goddess of healing and medicine. She at first shared this role with other healing goddesses, who eventually disappeared. Those ancient goddesses probably all had different responsibilities regarding healing, and as such they were often called all together in healing rituals:

In addition, the aid of an anonymous group of healing goddesses is called upon in Old Babylonian incantations: the seven and seven Daughters of Anu. They assist in the healing process by sprinkling soothing water from their pure vessels over the victims of disease, warding off eye trouble, skin diseases and inflammations, as well as over the mother in childbirth, to assist in a safe delivery. (Asher-Greve 2013, 85)

The two most powerful goddesses of healing, Bau and Gula, were eventually conflated. Before the constellation Lyra was associated with Bau, there is a mention that Vega was called Lamma, the messenger of Bau; in fact, Lamma, a female protective spirit, is indeed a messenger of the star Vega (Kurtik 2019, 343). Bau was known as a goddess from the earliest evidence, somewhere in the third millennium textual corpus. According to Kurtik, the goddess of healing and the constellation Lyra was primarily worshipped in Isin, an ancient Mesopotamian city, at the Exalted Palace temple and possibly in Umma, an ancient city of Sumer, both cities now in present-day Iraq. However, she was also revered under various names in numerous cities including Nippur, Ur, Uruk, Sippar, Larsa, Adab, and more. Over time, the attributes and functions associated with Gula were expanded to other Mesopotamian goddesses like Ninisina, Ninkarrak, Nintinuga, and Baba, who held significant importance in their own right (Kurtik 2019). All those goddesses eventually became associated with Gula.

Great goddess Bau had an autumn festival dedicated to her that lasted four days (Stuckey 2006). There, thousands of pilgrims came to offer her varied votives, many of them dog figurines. They received oracles in exchange for their gifts and of course healing of their ailments. The most important role that the goddess had during this festival was as a mediator between pilgrims and their ancestors and also gods and demons. Bau, as a chthonic deity, helped people connect with the dead. Healing goddesses always had the powers of necromancy and to prophesy (Stuckey 2006). The Sumerian king Gudea even chose Bau as his tutelary goddess, as he was very interested in dream divination. He was known for his dream interpretation and his extreme piety.

As a goddess of healing, Bau-Gula also had the power to inflict disease on others. Some incantations and even laws invoke her powers as a tool of vengeance against foes. Because she has liminal powers, being the guardian of thresholds, this goddess is often depicted on boundary stones. The boundary stones were laid down to protect temples and palaces. We usually find them underneath the Earth, where their powers could radiate throughout the buildings (Stuckey 2006).

As for the goddess Gula, the Temple of Isin, one of the greatest temples attached to Gula, attracted thousands of sick and dying people. Many came there to heal by the temple waters or for prayers and lamentations. What is exceptional is that thirty-three dogs were found buried at the temple (Stuckey 2006). They may have been sacrifices to the goddess, or perhaps there was a burial ground for sacred dogs that lived in the temple kennels. This temple is one of the few where dogs lived on site as the embodiment of the companion of the goddess. We will see how the dog is correlated to the Lyra constellation as well. Buried dogs were also found in Ashkelon where a temple dedicated to Aphrodite of the skies (Urania) was located and in Caria to a temple dedicated to Hecate. These examples reinforce the link between chthonic healing goddesses and dogs (Edrey 2008).

The association of the name Gula with the Vega star in the Mesopotamian textual corpus is more prevalent starting from the second millennium. The earliest specific mention of the name Gula with the constellation of Lyra dates from the seventeenth century BCE (Kurtik 2019). There we encounter various incantations using the constellation and the goddess name to give powers to medicine. It is indeed a particularly potent constellation to enhance medicinal plants. Many herbs were used in relation with astral irradiation (Reiner 1995, 15).

Bau-Gula, once merged together, was a goddess of regeneration; her words, the act of speaking, could generate life. The language of the ancient Mesopotamian priestesses was called *emesal*. This was a special dialect created for hymns and incantations toward the goddesses. It was known to be used only by women. Knowledge of plants and their magical language was used by those women, mostly priestesses and midwives, and they called upon the power of the goat star to make herbs more potent. This ancient constellation and divinity had many useful purposes; the knowledge of ancient women's magic has escaped history and it's up to us to try to uncover it.

Given that Bau was thought to be a regenerative goddess, a few scholars have assumed that she was connected with plant life. It makes total sense for two main reasons: (1) Plants are used in medicine and magic; and (2) stars are needed to help the plants become more effective. I would add that the tree, especially the palm tree and oak tree, as a symbol of life and regeneration, was linked to this type of goddess. You can find trees and goats in a lot of iconographies, especially those connected with Bau.

Bau also had dogs as companions. It was thought that dogs were messengers between the worlds and helped in healing. When she became syncretized as Gula, the dog figure followed her. Dogs are also thought to be guardians of the underworld, as we can see with the Egyptian Anubis and Greek Cerberus. But the dog is also present in the sky with its mistress under the name Sirius.

Here is an example of an incantation to Gula, the goat star:

> *Carnelian, lapis lazuli, yellow obsidian,* mekku, egizangu,
>   pappardilu, papparminu, lamassu?, *antimon, jasper,*
>   *magnetite,* turminu, abasmu, *twelve(sic!) stones (to*
>   *use) if a man has an "ill-wisher." . . . (you recite) the*
>   *incantation:*
> *O Bright one, let your angry heart be appeased,*
> *let your innermost relent, O Gula, exalted Lady.*
> *You are the one who created mankind, who bestows lots, food*
>   *portions, and food offerings,*
> *be present at my lawsuit, let me obtain justice through your*
>   *verdict,*
> *because of the sorceries, spittle and spatter, evil machinations*
> *of my adversary, let his evil doings turn back against him*
>   *and affect his head*
> *and his body, and I, your weary servant, will sing your*
>   *praises.*
>
> (REINER 1995, 128–29)

In this text, Gula is understood as a creatrix of mankind. She is invoked in an incantation against evil witchcraft and seems to be the judge of the plea, determining its veracity. If she agrees that the complaint is fair, she will punish the evildoer by causing sickness. This was common in ancient Mesopotamia. The use of magic was not prohibited, but it was not legal to use evil magic or sorcery. Is someone was unlucky it was believed that a witch, male or female, was responsible for this. This belief can be seen in the antiwitchcraft manuals widespread in the first millennium BCE, when conflicts about witchcraft seemed to have been quite common (Abusch 1987).

Ancient Gula was also capable of reversing illness, such as anxiety disorders, as this prayer attests. The "lifted-hand" mentioned in the last line was a gesture of powerful magic that was used when invoking a deity.

> O Gula, most exalted lady, who intercedes on behalf
>   of the powerless,
> With Marduk, king of the gods, merciful lord,
> Intercede! Speak a favorable word!
> May your wide canopy (of protection), your noble
>   forgiveness be with me.
> Provide a requital of favor and life for me,
> That I may proclaim your greatness (and) resound
>   your praises!
> It is the wording of a lifted-hand to Gula.
>   (LENZI 2011, 243)

Goddess Gula could intercede with any divinities for her followers. Great were her powers and her legacy endured for a long time. When her cult slowly changed, maybe into the Anatolian Hecate, the healing temples of Greece continued the legacy of astral bathing and healing. There the god Asklepius and his daughter Hygeia were renowned for their health-giving powers, and dogs were known to live in their temples or were even sacrificed to them (Ornan 2004, 18). Gula can be understood as a powerful energy that can be very efficacious and direct with her followers.

She can grant her wisdom and pity in the face of great illness, but she also is without mercy toward those who commit wrongful acts. You can rest assured that this ancient energy will not forget what has been done for her or what has been left undone.

ATAEGINA

The goddess Ataegina or Ataécina shares a lot in common with the healing goddess. Her name is similar to Aegina, the island that was the home of the warrior goddess Aphaia-Diktynna-Britomaris, although Ataegina and Aegina are not from the same language. Aegina was also known as a place of worship for Hecate. Ataegina is from the Iberian Peninsula, and her cult seems to have been quite important for the Lusitanians, who lived on the far west side of the peninsula. The etymology has many interpretations. J. Leite de Vasconcelos analyzed the name At(a)egina and suggested that it originated from Celtic roots. According to him, the prefix *ate* is similar to the prefix *re-* in English and Romance languages, indicating repetition or restarting. The root *gena* is comparable to the Latin word *genitus*, meaning "to give birth." Therefore, At(a)egina could mean "reborn" or "rebirth." Vasconcelos also mentioned a similarity to the Latin term *re-genita*, which also means "reborn." In simpler terms, At(a)egina's name could signify "the One (who is) Reborn," and Vasconcelos also suggested a link to *oíche*, the Gaelic word for "night" (Vasconcelos, 161–63). I think that this name and notion of being reborn at night fits this type of deity well, as ancient healing magic was always performed at night, under the auspicious eye of the dark skies.

This little-known goddess was linked with the goat figure, and scholars agree that she probably was an infernal deity, meaning her role was linked to the underworld. Given her association with the goat, this divinity most probably has a healing feature, which is indicated by the high number of votives offered to her. Therefore, Ataeagina shares all the features of the healing goddess of the night and death. I hope one day this divinity will be better understood and recognized for her fundamental function.

Present on funerary stelae and being a protector of birthing mothers, Ataegina may have also protected children. Here I have anecdotal evidence from someone who told me that in Portugal, the land where Ataegina was also an important goddess, it was common until the 1970s to dedicate a child to the moon. This person was the last one in his village to be a child of the moon. There, the families were performing rituals around a stone and by dedicating their child to the goddess, it was said that he would be protected by the moon all his life. There were three main conditions. These children had to continue the lineage of the family, plant a tree, and write a book. I am grateful to that person for the wonderful conversation that shed light on what I am exploring in this book—demonstrating how important the celestial world and goddesses have been for so long. Although here the moon was not linked to a specific goddess, it could be Ataegina or even a reminiscence of Tanit. Because most people in Portugal by that time were Christians, they only said that the moon was the protector of the child.

Sirius, Guardian of the Milky Way

I have explored the healing properties of the she-goat and the great goddesses Gula and Bau, and I have mentioned that they were always accompanied with dogs as one of their symbols. Sirius, nicknamed the Dog star, was and still is the second-brightest star in the night sky and the herald of the morning sun. Sirius, which can be seen at dawn just before the rising of the sun, is part of the constellation Canis Major. Canis Major is best seen on February 1st, the month that celebrates many female deities and spirits such as Brigid and her dog, the Basque lamiak, and Scandinavian female ancestors. For the Mesopotamians, this constellation was called the Bow and was eventually related to Inanna.

Although Gula's dog is not necessarily associated with Sirius, the Dog star, it is interesting to consider that dog lore is related to powerful healing goddesses, among them Sopdet. The ancient Egyptian name for the star Sirius was Sopdet, which was celebrated at the start of the Egyptian new year, just before the rising of the Nile. Personified as the goddess Sopdet, she was a psychopomp deity, meaning she brought the deceased to the underworld. In very late antiquity she was subsumed into Isis—as all goddesses were during that period.

Because Sopdet was associated with Sirius, the Dog star, during the later Ptolemaic and Roman period she was sometimes depicted as a dog or a woman sitting on a dog. Eventually, her male aspect transformed into Anubis. Her Greek equivalent was Sothis. Sirius is one of the three vertices of the Winter Triangle, the other two being Betelgeuse, which is part of the Orion constellation, and Procyon, which is in Canis Minor. Sirius is the brightest in the summertime. It is interesting that Sirius is associated with death, because dogs in proto-Indo-European lore are always guardians of the realm of the dead. Discoveries of dog remains in burial grounds of the Iron Age Wielbark culture and early medieval North-Western Slavs in Pomerania point to the enduring nature of this belief (Kajkowski 2015). It seems that dogs were often associated with the realm of the dead and some of them, such as Cerberus, even became its guardian. If the dog is linked to Sirius, we might wonder if Sirius is the protector of the realm of ancestors personified as the Milky Way.

It is said that when Sirius rises in late July and early August it marks the beginning of summer, announcing the very intense heat in the Mediterranean world. The term *canicula* is often used poetically or symbolically to refer to Sirius due to its association with the hot days of summer, as in many regions Sirius rises and sets with the sun during the hottest part of the year. In the Greek islands and during the Roman period, dogs were sacrificed to appease Sirius so that some cooler breeze would come. The Temple of Artemis of Eleusis is thought to have celebrated the culmination of Sirius at midnight just before the star disappears for seventy days. The link to Artemis here is interesting, first because she is often associated with Hecate and second because in the Sanskrit tradition, Sirius is seen as a deer hunter.

Sirius and the dog figure are incontestably linked to death. Literally because drought kills everything and metaphorically because the Sirius star guards the bridge to the underworld, which is the Milky Way. The Milky Way forms an arc resembling a bow or a bridge and Sirius—the "scorching light," the "torch" of the sky—is located in the middle, waiting for souls to come back home.

HECATE

A lot has been written about Hecate, and you can find very good literature about her history and development in the Greek world. Here, I mostly focus on the possibility that the Mesopotamian Gula-Bau may have given rise to Hecate. As noted earlier, in the creatrix chapter, Mary Bachvarova suggested that Hecate originated in the sun goddess of the Earth of the Hittite kingdom. Seeing that Hecate became a chthonic goddess, the solar origin does make sense. Bachvarova argues that Hesiod's prayers to Hecate are similar to the Hittite prayers to the sun goddess of Arinna, which we explored in the first chapter.

In earlier Greek texts, before the fifth century, there was no mention of Hecate's relation to witches, ghosts, and dark aspects. This could be a late addition to her cult as developed by the Greeks. She was though, early on, associated with gatekeeping, as this function is well established for sun deities. Even Apollo had the role to guard thresholds and entrances. This is typical because they are sun figures, and therefore their role is to chase away evil demons that live in darkness and on thresholds.

Because Hecate had a temple in Lagina, Anatolia, where she was revered as a savior and almighty mother, scholarship agrees, for now, that she might have originated in ancient Anatolia. Therefore, we cannot exclude that she might have had a Mesopotamian influence, given the proximity of the two cultures. Just like the healing goddess Gula, Hecate had dogs following her everywhere in art. I think this aspect too is linked to her association to the Mesopotamian healing goddess. Another Mesopotamian influence can be found in the Greek Magical Papyri, which consists of ancient spells written during the Greco-Egyptian period. In this corpus we can find a spell of protection against punishment that equates Hecate with the Mesopotamian goddess Ereshkigal, guardian of the underworld. The spell is named "Spell of Hecate Ereschigal against Fear of Punishment."

> If he comes forth, say to him: "I am Ereschigal, the one holding her thumbs, and not even one evil can befall her." If, however, he comes close to you, take hold of your right heel and recite the following: "Ereschigal, virgin,

bitch, / serpent, wreath, key, herald's wand, golden sandal of the Lady of Tartaros." And you will avert him "ASKEI KATASKEI ERŌN OREŌN IŌR MEGA SAMNYĒR BAUI (3 times) PHOBANTIA SEMNĒ." "I have been initiated, and I went down into the [underground] chamber of the Dactyls, and I saw / the other things down below, virgin, bitch, and all the rest." Say it at the crossroad, and turn around and flee, because it is at those places that she appears. Saying it late at night, about what you wish, it will reveal it in your sleep; and if you are led away to death, say it while scattering seeds of sesame, and it will save you. / "PHORBA PHORBA BRIMŌ AZZIEBYA." Take bran of first quality and sandalwood and vinegar of the sharpest sort and mold a cake. And write the name of so-and-so upon it, and inscribe it in such a way that you speak over it into the light the name of Hecate, and this: "Take away his sleep from such-and-such a person," and he will be sleepless and worried." (PGM LXX 1992, 4–25)

This association of Hecate with the underworld appears as early as the fourth century BCE in the Greek world. This is when she became associated with spirit magic and known as a goddess of witches.

Hecate's dog was also a symbol of the underworld. In the ancient world dogs were seen as chthonic creatures because they were always sniffing and digging into the ground, looking for buried things. As animals who would eat corpses and other dead animals, they were considered "impure" but also a strong symbol of the dead. This conflation of the goddess of death and goddess of healing and magic as being the ultimate role of Hecate can be found throughout Mesopotamian lore. Just like the Mesopotamian gods and goddesses who were thought to be the radiant light of the stars, Hecate has an epithet as bringer of light. That aspect may have come from her original role as a sun goddess of death and rebirth. Most bringers of light are sun deities, just like Apollo or even Artemis in one of her aspects. It is with no surprise that we find Hecate is often related to the Artemis that held sanctuaries to the deceased mothers. In the first chapter we investigated the role of the sun goddess of the underworld as a caretaker of the dead, especially of mothers and children.

And let us not forget that Hecate is the daughter of Asteria, the goddess of the stars. Therefore, as daughter of the stars, she can't be something other than a powerful star, a stellar object deemed important for the ancients. The celestial origins of Hecate as daughter of the stars and night sky and most radiant torch in the heavens is often overlooked. It was eventually believed that she would dwell as a sublunar spirit in Orphic spirituality. Therefore, she is the underworld solar goddess, and possibly Vega as well.

One other theory does associate Hecate with the goddess Lamashtu, who eventually became known as a demon. I say goddess here, because in the Lamashtu myth, she was indeed a goddess in the sky, the daughter of heaven, before being cast out and becoming a "demon" (West 1990).

Medicinal Herb Magic

The irradiation of the stars and constellations was well known in ancient Babylonia, and as such this method was used to reinforce the potency of the herbs. Many times, more than one star or constellation were named together as to accentuate the power given to the medicine. Indeed, as deities, they were often working in pairs or as a group in many rituals. Therefore the goat star is very often called upon at the same time as the Wagon (Ursa Major) and Venus. Assyriologist Erica Reiner noted that Gula as the goat star has many resemblances with Hecate in her manifestation as Selene. Both were called upon for healing ailments.

A healing deity such as Gula could also decide to give an illness to someone. In ancient times, incurable illnesses were considered a punishment from the divine world. The exorcist was supposed to find the deity that was angry to be able to perform a purification spell and the medical doctor would try his best to heal with medicinal herbs but they were not always able to heal a patient. In those cases, the patient was deemed to have received the hand of Gula. This hand of Gula was particularly associated with infants' illnesses, which is then suited to the roles that Greek goddesses held regarding the protection of young children. This negative aspect of the healing goddess Gula is reflected as a form of demonic aspect, which reinforces this idea that Hecate took on the role of Gula as a deity related to ghosts, demons, and witches.

Divinities of the ancient world, aka planets and constellations, had multiple aspects because they would not send off the same energy every day or even every season. Magic and amulets were used for this reason to prevent "demonic" energies, such as illnesses and bad luck sent from heaven, or to invoke the protective side of those energies. Again, this is an animistic worldview and the cosmic order was feared and revered by the ancients. They were very well aware of the influence that the astral world had on them.

GODDESS OF THE NIGHT

The Anatolian ancient cultures are probably less known by the general public. That is surprising because they probably had the most influence in Europe. It could be because the many kingdoms of Anatolia (the Hittites, Hurrites, Amorites, and so on) were under the cultural influence of Mesopotamia but also because the kingdoms died out and got forgotten like many others. These kingdoms had a divinity called the goddess of the night; scholars are not sure if she came from Mesopotamia or if she was an indigenous deity of the Hittites. Indeed, the Hittites are known to have been very tolerant of other cultures and they liked to import deities from their neighbors. Just like the Greeks, Hittites put their own view and interpretation on foreign gods and goddesses.

The goddess of the night is therefore an interesting case because this is an epithet that the Mesopotamians used to name the starry night sky. No single deity was known under that name. For the Hittites to call one particular goddess the goddess of the night is singular and worthy of mention. Researchers have been intrigued by this particular goddess, and many assumptions have been made. Her characteristics in Hittite texts show her to be an astral deity (Mouton 2004). She must be appeased as she can be easily angered. She seems to have links with oneiromancy, meaning that she is useful in dream divination and interpretation.

Some scholars have linked her to the Hittite goddess Shauska, associated with the planet Venus, who is an Ishtar-like goddess, but this association seems doubtful as the goddess of the night is mostly celebrated during moon festivals if she can be assimilated to the minor divinity called "night" in Hittite. The goddess of the night is mentioned alongside the Elamite goddess Pinikir, which is also linked to the warrior goddess Ishtar-Astarte. This was an important dyad in Hittite rituals. They both were sharing the same temple as well in certain cities. The fact that the goddess of the night shares aggressive aspect but also importance in dreams oracles and night rituals and that she is paired with the warrior goddess, we can maybe assume that the goddess of the night is the moon in the Hittite conception (Mouton 2004). It has been noted in fact that the moon aspect is also a quality found in Ishtar and Pinikir (Miller 2008).

That the moon is feminine is quite rare in the Near East but at the same time, all celestial objects had two genders and a dual aspect to them. The fact that we can't seem to find a moon goddess in ancient Mesopotamia and Levant doesn't mean that the Hurro-Hittite culture didn't have one. That could explain why goddesses originally from Anatolia eventually became associated with the moon (like Artemis and Hecate). Goddess of the Night is the best attribute we could give to the most visible astral object at night, which is the moon. Her physical aspects, according to one text, would have been that of a woman with a dog or lion head with wings. She is sometimes described as a black deity, but it could be mistranslated as she is more accurately a goddess of the night but not a dark goddess physically (Miller 2008). Therefore the symbols are related to the goddess of healing Gula.

Another role that the goddess of the night seems to have borne is possibly the protector of women about to give birth. She indeed appears in two prayers that ask to sanctify and protect women who are giving birth or are about to give birth. At least she is linked to a type of magic surrounding women. Queens and priestesses of the goddess of the night gave her golden jewelry, and they were almost always sanctified by blood sacrifices. She clearly was a difficult deity, demanding a lot of precious stones and metals (Mouton 2008). She was known to appear in dreams under her terrifying form, and a ritual called the Walkui ritual was meant to appease the person who would have seen the goddess in their dreams.

In the temples dedicated to her in at least three or four ancient cities, the goddess of the night statue was made entirely of gold. She would wear symbols of the sun and stars. She loved to receive as offerings fruits, legumes, and various herbs. She forbade the eating of pork, because it was associated with the underworld, in Hittite culture (and in the Mesopotamian culture as well). If the goddess of the night was not a moon deity, then she most likely was associated with death and the underworld. Those two aspects would indeed fit with rituals for birth, dreams, and healing. We still have not identified her yet but she could have had affinities with the healing goddess Gula that eventually reached the Anatolian soil as well.

For sure the goddess of the night was a star and considered as such, at least an astral object, a powerful one that was feared by queens and kings of the Hittite culture in the Bronze Age (Beal 2002). As a darkness deity just like the meteorite divinities, we have seen that solar deities and night deities are often linked in the conception of death and rebirth. Venus, moon, and underworld sun became an important feminine triad in the ancient world.

Here is a summary of how the goddess of the night would be worshipped:

A number of items of interest appear among the ritual paraphernalia. Besides the statue itself, the goddess has a gold sun disk called Pirinkir, a gold navel and a pair of gold *purka* (apparently a body part) inlaid with cast glass. These tiny objects have their own carrying case of stone inlaid with gold and semiprecious stones. Several of the goddesses' broaches are made of iron inlaid with silver (no doubt in niello technique), a reminder that in the second millenium, iron was still a precious metal. She is also provided with musical instruments, boxwood or ivory combs, two sets of clothing for her cross-dressing, an assortment of tables, chairs and footstools, and a small bronze basin to be used when she is bathed. Her privacy is to be protected with tapestries made from all five colors of wool and hung from bronze pegs fastened to either side of the entrance way to her courtyard. (Beal 2002, 202)

A Note about Ursa Major

Being the largest constellation in the sky, it is with no surprise the constellations of Ursa Major and Minor have played great roles in ancient religious history. For the Mesopotamian people it was called the Wagon. For the Celtic, Germanic, and Slavic people it is still called the Wagon and a great deal of lore has been made around that symbolism. Northern Europe has probably received the same cultural influence as the Hurrian and Hittite people for a while. The Sumerian goddess associated to the Wagon at first, was the goddess of the wind and of the underworld Ninlil. She was the merciful mother of the gods and chief of the Babylonian pantheon for a time.

The constellation of Ursa Major was understood as the binder of heaven and Earth and used in divination and healing magic. For example, alongside the goat star, irradiation of medicinal plants would enhance its properties in healing ailments as Assyriologist Erica Reiner explained: "Stars can be efficacious in healing illness since they may have been its cause. Poetic texts speak of illness from the udders of heaven or 'raining stars'; charms for protection against some illness it 'has come down from the stars in the sky'; from stars may be evil as well as beneficial, as 'dew of the stars' and the 'pure dew of the stars'" (Reiner 1995, 59). You could also harness the power of Ursa Major to inflict an illness on someone, although this kind of magic was forbidden in Mesopotamia. This constellation was eventually also equated with Inanna, so her powers could be cast all year long even when Venus was not visible (Reiner 1995). This constellation is also used in dream magic. Ursa Major can therefore be understood as a symbol of the night sky par excellence, because she never disappears. Being the Wagon she is also a symbol of the celestial barge that carries the gods (stars) and the souls to the skies. Carts, figuratively wagons, are also solar symbols of the underworld because they carry the sun underneath the Earth.

ARTEMIS-DIANA

For the Greeks, Ursa Major was seen as the bear, even though they knew of the name "the Wagon." I would like to explore its connection to Artemis. It was indeed well known that Artemis was assimilated to the bear but that she also was an aspect of the sun, being the sister of Apollo. Her cult at Brauron even included transformative rituals wherein young girls transformed into bears and danced under the starlight as a womanhood rite of passage (Papamichali et al. 2022). I like to think that they were dancing underneath Ursa Major in honor of the great weaver of life and healing constellation of the same name. Here is another example from the Greek Magical Papyri where we can see the bear as the celestial force of the goddess: "Bear, greatest goddess, ruling heaven, reigning over the pole of the stars, highest, beautiful-shining goddess, incorruptible element, composite of the all, all-illuminating, bond of the universe AEEIOYO (square)" (PGM IV 1992, 1275–1322).

Artemis-Diana cults were often linked to healing and protection of birthing mothers, particularly of dead children and mothers, another, yet not surprising, link to the importance of the goddesses in death. The cult of the healing Diana was widespread all over Europe, and she was a very important deity responsible for night rituals. She shared characteristics with the Greek Artemis as a lunar figure as well, as they became conflated as one under the Roman rule.

One of the most important places of worship for Diana was at Nemi, where she was the goddess of healing (Nemorensis). Young virgins and priestesses were amassing oak wood to keep her temple fires burning. In what is now Switzerland she was associated with the goddess Artio, the bear goddess, reinforcing her role as the healing bear goddess whose cult was very important to the local population.

Finally, Diana eventually became associated with the night goddess Hecate and so became known as the goddess of witches and witchcraft, just like Hecate. In European folklore, Diana is an enduring figure from the women's mysteries.

☙ *Facing Vulnerability* ❧

The message of the healing goddess is this one: To heal you must present your vulnerability. Thus revealing our true self is the harder aspect of ourselves to show to the world. You must be able to let the walls down and give your heart to the cosmos. What is unhealthy in your life? What part of your body and heart needs healing? To heal you also must forgive your past and forgive your lineage. Female wounds are often passed down from generation to generation, and the healing goddess calls on us to confront them and heal them. The healer is an energy of regeneration. Existential rebirth is possible when the past is left alone where it belongs. The healing process takes time, just like the regeneration of nature does.

HOW TO WORK WITH

The Healer

The best time to work with the healer constellations and stars are during the summer solstice and the winter solstice. Rituals held for those deities are always done at night and in the darkest place possible. The best incense and plants for these energies are essence of oak and incense made of wood resin. Always give them as offerings under the smoke form.

Healing is the most difficult journey we can encounter. Sometimes it takes a lifetime; we often need to repeat the healing process throughout our lives. What follows are simple ways to heal the many wounds of the heart and soul.

Traditionally, rituals held for Gula or Hecate were done during the night near a fire and a lake, under the auspicious Vega star. The lake at night is a dark mirror that reflects the sky, a portal to the divine world. If you cannot sit by a dark lake at night, find a black mirror and use it to ask yourself what is unhealthy in your life and what you want to get rid of. Write down your answers on paper and then burn the paper. It is especially good to do this ritual on dark moon days.

You can also access the healing power of these goddesses in the very early hours of the morning. In ancient times, our ancestors would wake up after four hours of sleep to do creative work, to meditate, or to pray and then would go back to sleep for another four hours. We were biologically in tune with the dark skies, and we still wake up during the night. If you experience this, try to make the best of it and make music or meditative sounds. It will resonate in the universe. Nighttime is also the best time for dream divination with Vega, as will be explored in the chapter on celestial healing.

Finally, another method to make sure you heal and stay protected is to wear an amulet that is dedicated to one of the goddesses explored in this chapter. This amulet must be infused with the moon and star energies for three nights in a row. Use a prayer or incantation and ask for the energies to stay in that amulet. Repeat the process after a few months.

Flight of the Swan Maiden, by John D. Batten, 1919

THE LADY
OF THE SEA

Inanna, Astarte, Aphrodite-Urania,
Tanit, Atargatis, Nanshe

Celestial Bodies: Deneb, moon, Venus, Cygnus
Symbols: Swan, cypress
Seasons: February to September
Symbolic Message: Transformation

The moon is rightly believed to be the star of the spirit
that saturates the earth and fills bodies by its approach
and empties them by its departure
the blood even of humans increases and diminishes
*   with its light*
and leaves and herbage are sensitive to it
the same force penetrating into all things.

PLINY IN ALLEGRO 1970, 70

Venus, the brightest star in the sky that appears after sunset and just before sunrise, has historically been a powerful symbol for many cultures. This star has always represented a powerful goddess with both masculine and feminine aspects. But Venus is almost always working alongside other celestial objects, such as the moon and the star Deneb from the Cygnus or Swan constellation. In many ancient religions, Friday was linked to the planet Venus and was considered a sacred day of the goddess for this reason. As an enduring divine power, the ancient figures that we explore in this chapter were more complex than what we usually think. Let us see how the powerful swan maiden is still relevant for us.

The night sky offers us a spectacular rendering of our place in the cosmos. There is no better way to feel one with the Earth than when you feel so small before the greatness of the ever-expanding universe. A particular cluster of stars, the Cygnus constellation, was once perceived as our ancestral home and the path our souls take after death leading the way to the Milky Way. The Milky Way was once connected to the dove or to waterbirds like the swan. In today's Irish folklore, for example, it was believed that the swans or other types of birds were associated with tombs and death; hence many sites in Ireland could be linked to the Cygnus constellation.

The significance of this constellation and the emblematic swan figure extends beyond European cultures to include the Mediterranean and Eastern civilizations. Sharing the same northern celestial hemisphere, the ancient inhabitants of the Mediterranean were influenced by the cosmic narratives woven into the stars. As we explore this rich tapestry, we will encounter some of the most prominent feminine figures from the ancient Mediterranean world. In this chapter, we delve into the profound connection between the celestial queens of the heavens, the Moon, Venus, and the star Deneb, examining their roles as protectors of women and children, and guiding souls into the realm of the afterlife.

The goddesses that I present in this chapter were also very often associated with Venus. But her role and function as a powerful planet have been obliterated by, yet again, reductive roles, personifying beauty and lust. The reason behind this is because of the prevalence of the naked feminine motif on plaques and amulets that were found almost everywhere in the ancient Near East. These nude figures have been interpreted as symbols of fertility and identified as diverse representations of Venus such as Inanna or Astarte. As we will see, the lady of the sea, as I call her, was more than a passive figure of love.

The Greeks equated almost all of the Eastern goddesses with Aphrodite, who is herself not originally from Greece (Budin 2004, 96). The Mediterranean protective goddess was one of the most popular and powerful figures to have survived. She offered help in various areas of life but was mainly a transformative healing deity, a guide to the ancestors, and a protector of seafarers. I am not convinced that every one of these goddesses is a manifestation of Venus. The relation to Deneb and the moon seems to be far more important, as I will discuss. These goddesses are also representations of the dawn—that liminal time and space between Earth and the sky—and as such they bring forth their lunar aspect. The moon, just like the sun, was a male figure in the ancient Near East; his lunar aspect was mostly linked to the waxing moon and its fertile energy. The waning and full moon were more a matter of female energy and healing powers. The moon and its associated divinities were therefore dual gendered and transformed into male or female, depending on the time of day and day of the month. Although Venus was also a dual energy, there is much to be said about how nineteenth-century scholars "Venusified" the ancient goddesses, but that is beyond the scope of this book. Before plunging into the temples of our main figure, I would like to explore a little constellation that is very often forgotten.

The Legend of Corona Borealis

There is a magical constellation that tends to be forgotten when we look at the sky. Even researchers, when trying to understand the astral equivalent of deities, do not think about the wonderful Corona Borealis. This little constellation is the subject of many legends around the world and is often associated with dancing maidens. The constellation is made up of seven stars that move around in the heavens. One of the oldest goddesses associated with this constellation is the Sumerian goddess Nanaya. She was known under many epithets such as "Divine Seven of Elam" and "Lady of the princely powers, emerging brilliantly like the daylight, chosen forever for her virtuous beauty" (Black et al., 2.5.1.3, 1–4). She was an important goddess in many cities of the Sumerian kingdom and was still important afterward in the expansion of the Akkadian and Assyrian kings. She continued to be a venerated goddess until the seventh century CE in Iran and even India. Though her roles and function have largely been forgotten today, she was one of the goddesses that had the longest enduring worship.

Nanaya's function was interesting because she was a goddess linked to royalty and justice (Metcalf 2019, 70). More specifically she was responsible for giving land to princes and princesses. Because this constellation is in the shape of a crown or a crescent moon, she is often conflated with Venus and the moon. Being quite shiny in the sky, she is often referred to as beautiful. In her many hymns dating before the first millennium, she is attested as the one who weaves humanity together and the bringer of victory to her people. As exemplified here, she was considered important to the people who looked upon her light for their wishes: "Laughingly, a word of joy, he said to her, making her heart radiant: 'You rule over the world's inhabitants! The people look upon you(!), upon your light, as (at) the sun's!'" (Streck and Wasserman 2012, 189). As a giver of kingship and land, she gave, in a ritual, bronze arrows to the god Bel to legitimize him as the tutelary god of Arbela.

Nanaya was described as sometimes having a beard in some cities or many breasts in others. In the first millennium she was assimilated into Inanna, although this is now disputed as Nanaya is clearly her own goddess. During Hellenistic times she was equated with Artemis. She is associated with Corona Borealis in astronomical texts (Stol 1998).

The ancient Greeks called this constellation Ariadne's Crown. In Greek mythology, Princess Ariadne, after escaping her father, King Minos, ran off with Theseus to an island. Dionysus appeared on the island, stole the beautiful Ariadne from Theseus, and married her. After her death, Dionysus placed the crown of Ariadne (Corona Borealis) among the stars to honor her. The function of Corona Borealis as giver of kingship has also survived in European legends. In Welsh mythology, Corona Borealis was the celestial home of Arianrhod, a goddess who gives titles and lands and weaves destiny. All of these figures became associated with the sea and birds. Corona Borealis is therefore a bringer of divine kingship and good fortune to those who work with her and is our guide to the land of the souls.

INANNA

Inanna is a very ancient deity, and one who eventually transcended all other goddesses for millennia until Isis took her place. She was so powerful that she was associated with many constellations. For this reason, it is difficult to choose which category or chapter she fits in. She took on the roles of many ancient goddesses, and she could have been the warrior or the healer, but I think that as an ancestress of the lady of the sea, Inanna is an enduring figure even in today's religions.

Great Inanna is a complex figure, and I always felt she was misunderstood; in fact, all of these sex and warrior goddesses who are "ladies of the sea" have had their histories misinterpreted. When studying in France at the Maison de l'Orient et de la Méditérranée, I learned that lapis lazuli was attributed to Inanna and that her eyes were very often made of lapis lazuli. According to my late professor, that meant that Inanna was related to the night sky and resurrection because lapis was used for deities found in tombs.

Inanna was not always associated with the planet Venus; it seems this attribute was added later in her history. The first attestation for the planet Venus comes from the Sumerian goddess Ninsianna. She was called the Red Lady of Heaven in Old Babylonian. Like other goddesses associated with this planet, she was seen as a female in the morning and a male in the evening, following the movements of the planet Venus. It is with no surprise that she was eventually absorbed into Inanna and later Ishtar, who was the most popular goddess in the second millennium BCE.

Inanna is attested in Sumer from the fourth millennium BCE. She was at first represented as a reed pole. The poles were placed in front of temples, just like some contemporary shamanistic totems today. The cuneiform symbols attest that her name originally was associated with burial mounds or maybe some sort of transitional space, as the poles indicate. Professor Johanna Stuckey defined Inanna as a goddess of transitions in life: "What unifies Inanna is change—transformation and transition. She is the way in and the way out, the door, the gateway. What more appropriate symbol for her than gateposts? Forever an adolescent poised at the threshold of full womanhood, maiden Inanna was the eternal threshold through which everything passed in fulfillment of the cycle that is life" (Stuckey 2004, 6).

This analysis corresponds to the vision I have of the original Inanna, before she was syncretized with the warrior goddess Ishtar. Her role with death is very often overlooked and misunderstood, and as an eternal virgin, interchangeably male or female, she is indeed a figure that links both worlds. That tells me that she had a link with death, or the transition toward it. Being there for the general population as a powerful symbol of transformation, from life to death and regeneration, she clearly gained political powers with the kings. Inanna is a goddess of the twilight, the zone between heaven and Earth, just below the ocean, where the souls dwell. This belief was described by Plato as it was still a common conception during his lifetime. Hecate was also believed to dwell in this sublunar zone, the twilight and liminal space just before the sun descends into the underworld. Dedicated hymns to Inanna also inform us of how she was perceived at dawn during this twilight period, which could be a reference to the crown, Corona Borealis, or, of course, Venus.

> Lady of all the divine powers, resplendent light, righteous woman clothed in radiance, beloved of An and Urac! Mistress of heaven, with the great pectoral jewels, who loves the good headdress befitting the office of en priestess, who has seized all seven of its divine powers! My lady, you are the guardian of the great divine powers! You have taken up the divine powers, you have hung the divine powers from your hand. You have gathered up the divine powers, you have clasped the divine powers to your breast. Like a dragon you have deposited venom on the foreign lands. When like Ickur you roar at the earth, no vegetation can stand up to you. As a flood descending upon (?) those foreign lands, powerful one of heaven and earth, you are their Inana. (Black et al. 4.07.2, 1–12)

The symbol of her reed post standing in front of the temple was also used for celestial bathing in ancient Mesopotamia. Reed was a sacred material used for many things. In ancient Egypt, the reed fields were associated with the afterlife. We could assume it was the same for ancient

Mesopotamian. This could explain how ancient Inanna was related to death. Much like the cults of Gula or Hecate, Inanna was linked to possession rites in ancient temples; as her counterpart, Ishtar could have been the mediator between the world of the gods and humans. Priests were involved in her cult and were "possessed" by her, who would then bring them messages from the divine world (Stuckey 2008, 7).

Another feature from the archaic Inanna was her association with doves. It is said in some ancient texts that Inanna received many doves as sacrifices such as votive offerings made of bronze, and sometimes she also received sacrifices of real doves. Doves were used in funerary practices in the ancient world and were known to make shrieking sounds when grieving. Sounds of grief are also a feature of Inanna, for she is a keening goddess when death is near. As such, we can understand her as a timeless force that announces coming doom and grief, for in many cultures a similar spirit or goddess would appear when someone is close to death.

As an agent of death and war, in Mesopotamian lore she is sometimes described as fierce and cruel and even scary in her warrior aspect. She could transform into a bird of prey, as explored in the warrior chapter.

> Inana, a falcon preying on the gods . . . To keep paths and ways in good order, to shatter earth and to make it firm are yours, Inana. To destroy, to build up, to tear out and to settle are yours, Inana. To turn a man into a woman and a woman into a man are yours, Inana. Desirability and arousal, goods and property are yours, Inana. Gain, profit, great wealth and greater wealth are yours, Inana. Gaining wealth and having success in wealth, financial loss and reduced wealth are yours, Inana. Observation (1 ms. has instead: Everything), choice, offering, inspection and approval are yours, Inana. Assigning virility, dignity, guardian spirits, protective deities and cult centres are yours, Inana. (Black et al., 4.07.3, 29–38, 115–31)

In this invocation, all of her roles are described and merged, and we understand that she was a lot to deal with. She is named frequently as the Lady of Sealands, and when she was not in a good mood, she was responsible for darkening the skies. This could be referring to eclipses, as in: "darkening the bright daylight, she turns midday into darkness" (Black et al., 4.07.3, 49–59). As a fierce light, her astral fire would light the path in the sky: "Your torch lights up the corners of heaven, turning darkness into light" (Black et al., 4.07.3, 209–18).

In light of these examples, it seems that Inanna is mostly related to twilight and possibly dawn. She could be a representation of the evening star and of the dusk itself, as the celestial gods could not work without the night sky. The night sky was, after all, in many cultures a distinct goddess. She seems to be related to the full and dark moon. The fact that she could be associated with the moon is also related to her cult as she is said to have died and come back after three days (like the moon) in the myth of her descent. Venus is also known for dying as the evening star and being reborn as the morning star. Her astral aspect and political importance is reflected in many myths, one that I particularly like is a hymn that shows how her symbolic father gave her powers, probably reflecting when she received functions from other deities.

> My father has given me the sky, has given me the earth: The Lady of the Heaven am I. Will anyone, any God, match me? [. . .] The war he has given to me, the din of battle he has given to me, the hurricane he has given to me, the whirlwind he has given to me. The sky he put as crown on my head, the earth he put as sandal beneath my foot, the gleaming coat of the gods he put around me [. . .] The sky is mine, the earth is mine—I am the Lady-Hero! (Falkenstein 1953: 67–68)

Once again, here we can see the dark aspects of Inanna, how turmoil such as storms and wars are brought forth to explain her chaotic nature. She wears the sky as a crown and walks on the earth as if it were her sandals. She wonders if other gods could be as important as her—and indeed, she did receive an enduring cult.

In the famous literary text that relates the descent of Inanna into the underworld, the tale that possibly influenced the myth of Demeter and Persephone, Inanna departs from her main cities. She literally removes her presence, the "me" (divine radiance) in her main temples, and she brings this radiance with her into the underworld. There she meets her sister Ereshkigal, queen of the dead, and is killed by demons. She gets resurrected but in exchange for another life, the life of her consort Dumuzi. Inanna has many aspects, which is evident in the poem, where she takes her seven presences from the temples. Once again, seven is an important symbolic number for ancient Mesopotamian, and it also represents many important celestial objects, such as the seven Pleiades stars or even the seven main planets and Corona Borealis. As such, Inanna's descent into the underworld could be interpreted as an initiatic journey into the world of grief, a trance state that could be attained by performing shamanistic rituals.

The story of her descent was thought for a long time to be an agricultural tale. But if you look into it more, it describes the movements of the stars, as exemplified here: "The journey of Inanna through the seven cities describes a route from south to north and from east to west, which may be related to the movement of the celestial bodies through the sky. In the Mesopotamian pantheon, the astral deities such as Nanna and Inanna were linked to the movement and the cyclical disposition of the cosmic development" (Cabrera 2018, 57).

Inanna is often accompanied by her servant, the vizier named Ninshubur, a female deity who serves as the messenger of the gods and accompanies Inanna on her journeys. Some scholars suggest that Ninshubur could be represented by Orion. Similar to Inanna, Ninshubur's gender varies, reflecting the shifting celestial energies. While typically depicted as female alongside Inanna, Ninshubur is occasionally portrayed as male when aiding An, the sky god. As a warrior deity, Inanna embodies both genders, each highlighting different facets of her nature, eventually earning her the title of the goddess of sex and war.

It's crucial to note that the concept of "love" associated with Inanna is not romantic but rather rooted in sexual magic and desire. Many depictions identified as Inanna portray her displaying her genitals, a gesture intended to intimidate enemies, kings, and even demons. In the ancient world, female genitalia were believed to hold significant power. The vulva was viewed as a gateway to potent forces of libidinal magic, often instilling fear in men. Inanna, however, embraces the power of eroticism, asserting herself as the mistress of the vulva (Serwint 2002, 329). Across various cultures, the act of exposing the genitals or buttocks, known as *anasyrma*, was employed as apotropaic magic to ward off evil, demonstrating that feminine sexuality is a strong force—a force that the patriarchy would eventually feel the need to control.

I must say, though, that Inanna has many attributes that correlate with the ancient goddesses of the night sky. In fact, she is associated with many stellar objects because of her growing importance. She is thought to be a form of the star Sirius, named the Bow (Sirius) and also the constellations the Wagon (Ursa Major), Virgo, and the Lion. And of course, she is also related to the constellation Pisces (White 2014). These different aspects of the great goddess Inanna represent the great powers she held and the variety of magic she could produce from these different stars. As we have explored, her association with the realm of the dead and to Sirius is probably her dark aspect linking her to her sister Ereshkigal. The triple nature of the gods, as I earlier explained, was quite common.

Inanna eventually became equated with the Akkadian Ishtar, who was as ferocious as Inanna. The name Ishtar was associated with the Canaanite Athartu (Astarte), a deity closely associated with the South Arabian Semitic astral god Athtar, who was believed to embody the planet Venus, which was the brightest star in the desert sky. It is noteworthy that in South Arabia, Venus was considered to be male, while Ishtar was sometimes referred to as the "Lady with the Beard." Her dual gender was a characteristic shared by Ishtar, Astarte, and occasionally Aphrodite. It is important to emphasize that Ishtar was always regarded as a warrior and a protective figure, despite her ability to influence love and relationships and male impotence. In the ancient world, there is no mention of her having a specific role in motherhood and fertility. Nevertheless, her popularity among kings, young warriors, and sailors remained significant.

ASTARTE

To understand the Phoenician world and their important goddess Astarte, one must first understand the Ugaritic kingdom, which helped shape religions around the Mediterranean. The Ugaritic kingdom was located in today's Syria, and it is the culture that most influenced the ancient Hebraic people who wrote the Old Testament.

Astarte was at first a warrior maiden goddess whose sister is the goddess Anat. They appear together in the Ugaritic literature of the Late Bronze Age. Since Anat was more important and received an important cult, Astarte played a minor role in the religions of Ugarit until she was imported into the Egyptian pantheon along with her sister. Astarte was a warrior goddess known to ride horses (Schmitt 2013, 223). She was also one of the patron goddesses of the Egyptian pharaoh Ramses II. Astarte is one of the most misinterpreted ancient goddesses. She is still widely viewed as a fertility and sexual goddess, but if we look closely at her iconography and her roles in ancient textual sources, there are very few mentions of active sexuality or fertility. Astarte was originally depicted as a young warrior maiden and huntress. She is known in the Ugaritic cycles for her rage, just like her sister Anat. The riding Astarte had a very important connection to royalty. She was the figure who would legitimize the king. In that role, as a warrior and protectress of royalty, she became, with Anat, an important goddess in the Egyptian kingdom during the Late Bronze Age. Many scarabs were inscribed with the names of Astarte and Anat in the context of war (Schmitt 2013, 224). We find phrases naming her as Mistress of Heavens or Lady of the Sea. The association with the sea, as I will demonstrate, is an important feature here. West Asian deities, such as Anat, Astarte, and the god Reshep from Ugarit and other Syro-Phoenician cities, were incorporated into the Egyptian pantheon during the Fifteenth Dynasty. The tale of Astarte and the sea, found on the papyrus Amherst, is a version of the tale found in West Semitic texts of Ugarit about a battle with Yamme the sea and the goddess Astarte (Stadelmann). Of course, Astarte was not only a warrior goddess, like her counterpart Ishtar; she was also revered in Egypt as a goddess of healing and magic (Schmitt 2013, 224).

Her association with horses is quite interesting because this probably reflects ancient funerary customs. We indeed find iconography of Astarte on war plates worn by horses, and oracular texts mention her association with this animal. She is called Lady of the Chariots. Most of the Egyptian and Syrian iconography from the Bronze Age depicts her riding horses with bows and arrows. She sometimes will also stand over a lion, like Ishtar. Definitely the horse is uniquely an Astarte symbol (Cornelius 2008). Horse symbolism very often refers to the animal that rides before the sun or the moon. As such, they are symbols of the dawn, the land of the souls. The horse also pulls the heavenly cart that carries souls to the land of no return. In ancient Mesopotamia, the dead were transported in wagons, or at least the nobility were. Inanna was also associated with the Wagon (Ursa Major), and she is thought to have influenced the cult of Astarte on the Mediterranean side. In many north European cultures, the wagon is a symbol of the death cart riding toward the home of the souls. For me Astarte was probably a very ancient form of the Valkyries, female figures who rode on horseback, carrying the souls of fallen warriors to Valhalla. This was probably her original role before being syncretized with other goddesses during the Iron Age. She kept her function as a goddess of royalty and as a caretaker of the dead and of rebirth, but her warlike aspect diminished with time.

She played a significant role for the Phoenicians. It might have been because she was first their prime goddess that she eventually was known in Ugarit—but she was not very significant there compared to Anat. Both Astarte and Anat appeared as healing figures for snake bites and Astarte is conjured as an apotropaic and healing figure against all kinds of evil (Lewis 2011, 216). The fierce nature of the goddess is of very good help to protect against ailments. The first millennium BCE saw the rise of Astarte in many kingdoms, and with the fall of Ugarit, her sister Anat was slowly forgotten.

In the Phoenician world, her cult spread widely under the name of Baalat-Gubal, which meant the Lady of Byblos. Byblos was an important commercial city located in today's Lebanon. The very cosmopolitan cities of the ancient Palestinian territories, such as Tyre and Sidon, witnessed the presence and cults of many people from all around the ancient world, mostly Egyptians, Arameans, Mesopotamians, and Hittites. It was customary to offer hair to Astarte. Some texts mention that pilgrims would go to the Astarte temple and offer their hair in exchange for her blessings and protection (Karageorghis 2003). Hair was considered to be a magical force and to represent the epitome of human divinity and was therefore a good offering, especially before marriage. The Phoenicians accorded a great importance to death, ancestor worship, and divinities related to death, which must be why Astarte was their beloved deity.

With the Phoenician expansion within the Mediterranean in the first millennium, Astarte gradually became associated with the Cypriot Kypris, as demonstrated here:

> Her violent aspect, still present in the first part of the 1st Millennium BCE, receded more and more into the background during the second part of the 1st Millennium. This was probably due to her character as a goddess of royalty and kingship, which gradually transferred her warlike qualities to masculine deities. In the westward Phoenician expansion she would become a more universal high goddess, merging with local deities and taking on similar political functions like Aphrodite/Kypris, thereby strengthening her aspect/role/status as a major female deity. The high goddess's aspect as a healing deity would persist into the Hellenistic-Roman Period. (Schmitt 2013, 224)

Apart from the horses, the symbols of Astarte were also birds, especially doves and swans (Marinatos 2000, 38). In ancient incantations, Venus and the moon often accompany other stars and constellations in their transitions, so it seems likely the combination of both forces was required to accomplish the rituals that were held for healing and protective patronage of transformation.

She is associated with the sea because swans are waterbirds. Many accounts in her myths shows her triumphing over the sea, as in the Ugaritic texts. She probably was understood as a strong force against the many dangers of the sea. Many Astarte amulets were found in shipwrecks so we know that sailors sought protection from this goddess. It is most probably, according to some scholars, the reason why the Catholic Virgin Mary has been associated with seaside towns and as a patron of sailors. Some even consider Mary to be the continuation of the cult of Astarte, which was prominent for a while (Benko). Of course, Mary as the "mother of God" was a Queen of Heaven. Mary, as it is clear now, shares similar aspects and is related to the star of the sea (Venus) whose epithet demonstrates her importance in guiding and protecting people at sea and at their seaside cities.

APHRODITE-URANIA

Aphrodite-Urania (heavenly Aphrodite) was thought to be the Eastern Astarte in her Greek version from the fourth century BCE. As such she was sometimes called the Syrian Aphrodite (Vianu 1997). Being that the cult of Astarte was spread all over the Mediterranean world, it's no surprise that she reached the island of Cyprus, where it was said that Aphrodite was born. Cyprus is an isolated island that seemed to have evolved on its own from 5000 to 3000 BCE (Karageorghis 1977). Eventually, traders and merchants from the Anatolian, Syro-Mesopotamian, and Cretan worlds began to settle and trade there. There was already a local cult associated with female figures on the island, but little is known about it. We know that Kypris was receiving a cult there and also the Wanassa, a goddess or a woman of royalty. At first it was proposed that the Cypriots had ancestor cults just like the rest of the civilizations around them (Karageorghis 1977).

During the Bronze Age period, many female figures found on Cyprus had a bird-like face, many holding children. Here I can only presume that we can see the relations with the solar symbol of the bird of prey and the legitimization of children's royalty by that goddess. Or perhaps it was related to the protection of children and mothers. In any case, until the coming of the Phoenicians to the island, there are no texts that can help us interpret those goddesses of that period, if they are goddesses. It is when religious syncretism happens that sometimes we have a way to tell how other cultures understood these deities from outside their countries. The many names and epithets that were found on the island indicate that there was a "queen," Mycenean Wanassa, showing that an important goddess worship was already in place before Aphrodite came to be known on this island (Sugimoto 2014).

There is no doubt that there were many local manifestations of different goddesses on Cyprus. As per all cities of the ancient world, they eventually became one "great goddess" associated with the most popular one. It was showed clearly that Aphrodite was a late import on the island of Cyprus (Sugimoto 2014, 207).

In nearly all her sanctuaries on the island, she was venerated as a Copper Baetyl. The representation of the goddess in these sanctuaries deviated from the human form and took the shape of a circular block, resembling a cone that gradually narrows from the bottom to the top: "The image of the goddess does not bear the human shape; it is a rounded mass rising like a cone from a broad base to a small circumference. The meaning of this is doubtful" (Tacitus 1942, 2.3). This is very much like the goddess Tanit, as will be discussed next.

What about the association with Astarte? Aphrodite and Astarte evolved as different goddesses—Astarte being a war deity and Aphrodite whose reign was over relationships and desire—and ended up taking the features of the great goddesses of the Near East. They evolved together in the Mediterranean world, but they were not the same deities at first. They ended up being fused together by the fifth century BCE (Budin 2004, 127).

Where was she worshipped? One of the places associated with the Astarte-Aphrodite cult was a cavern located in Lebanon. Many offerings were left in the cavern, and some Greek inscriptions in it suggest that she was a patron of the king and his sons and was thanked for healing the people. This place was eventually turned into a Virgin Mary sanctuary (Beaulieu and Mouterde). As we can see, the enduring powers of the goddess Astarte are still present through the Virgin Mary sanctuaries; just like Astarte, visiting Mary in her caverns will bring health and prosperity to those praying to her. Her worship reached many places, spreading as far as the Black Sea.

The celestial aspect of Aphrodite survived through her form known as Urania, the goddess of the starry sky, as Urania was seen as the daughter of the sky, and the swan was her symbol. The many epithets of Aphrodite could refer to her many associations with the different goddesses, whom she obtained through time. Also, as I have already mentioned, there are very often three aspects to ancient goddesses, such as sky, sea, and Earth. Therefore, some cults were more prevalent on some aspects than others.

She ended up taking many celestial forms:

> The erratic pattern of the morning and evening star alternately rising
> in conjunction with the moon and setting in conjunction with the sun
> may explain why the ancients saw Aphrodite as both a celestial goddess
> and goddess of the underworld. Her association with an older moon
> goddess during her celestial phase linked her with the tidal cycles and
> hence her connection with the sea. The violence of her birth through
> interaction between the elements air (masculine) and water (feminine)
> through violent agitation (foam) indicates that she was born from
> both love and violence, and could be a goddess of love and vengeance.
> (Mccary in Manning 2015, 8)

The association of Aphrodite with the celestial sky and the moon
indicates to me that the ancient cults of the ancestors survived through her
as she transformed and adapted herself from the Near Eastern cultures to
the Greek culture. Her association with the moon, which is both male and
female, brought into perfect harmony the energies required for divination
and protection.

TANIT

Tanit is an enigmatic and interesting ancient goddess who still has
influence in the Mediterranean cultures. For me, she is an ancient celestial
force who is retelling us the importance of honoring our ancestors. Some
scholars associate this Carthaginian goddess with a representation of the
goddess Astarte. Tanit was brought to North Africa by the Phoenicians
during the Roman expansion. She had the same functions as the typical
lady of the sea that Astarte had. She was a protector of cities, mariners,
and children. Her iconography was simpler, though: a simple triangle with
a circle as the head and the arms posing up toward the sky. This posture
is similar to that of the goddesses on Cyprus. There is most probably a
syncretism here with Astarte and a local goddess from North Africa
(Stuckey 2009b). She was thought to have a luminescent gemstone on her
forehead, making the temple bright at night, a symbol of her astral origin.

When you look at the sky, you can see that Venus is sometimes located inside the crescent of the moon, which is the symbol that Tanit wears. The star within a crescent moon was called the sign of Tanit. Its meaning is similar to the Egyptian ankh symbol, which signifies eternal life. The sign of Tanit is sometimes linked with the word *mirror* as well. This symbol most often appears on sarcophagi and tombs, marking its inevitable link to the underworld.

Tanit priestesses were described in some ancient texts as performing the dance of the stars. It was considered an astronomical dance, an earthly manifestation of the movement of the celestial sky. This reflects the ancient religious belief that certain movements and sounds could reproduce the ancient celestial dance that gave us life. We are still moved by these ancestral energies, which is why chants and dance are sacred arts. Although associated with Astarte, Tanit was also known in late antiquity as a lunar goddess, reinforcing the idea that Astarte was originally perceived as a lunar goddess. Lucian mentions that Astarte is a moon goddess in his work: "There is likewise in Phœnicia a temple of great size owned by the Sidonians. They call it the temple of Astarte. I hold this Astarte to be no other than the moon-goddess" (Lucian 1913, 44). Hence, both Tanit and Astarte are understood to be related to different celestial powers and phases of the moon.

The goddess Tanit was even associated by the Romans to the North African Cealestis, who was very popular. This equation makes more sense to me; although the war figures such as Inanna-Ishtar-Astarte are said to be Venus, they also have a lunar aspect, as we have seen, because they share underworld solar characteristics and healing properties. They are closely linked to death and regeneration and linked to the ancestors. Tanit had an important cult in Spain at Ibiza. In Cornwall, according to a legend, she would have been recognized under the name Tanat. Being the main goddess of Carthage, many children were offered to Tanit. It could be because of her association as a protector in death and that grieving mothers would put their departed infants under her protection. It makes me think about the story of the children dedicated to the moon in Portugal, which I mentioned earlier. The founder of the magical practice Wicca, Gerald

Gardner, is said to be buried in Tunis, the land of the goddess Tanit, guardian of the deceased.

ATARGATIS

Atargatis is an ancient goddess from the Roman and Hellenistic periods and was known to be a form of Aphrodite and Astarte. Since her appearance is quite late in antiquity (about fourth century BCE), she was sometimes solely known under the name of the Syrian goddess (Dea Syria). Her iconography was quite unusual as she was depicted having a fishtail and looking like a mermaid. The doves were sacred to her, as per her connection to the other Mediterranean goddesses. Indeed, Atargatis could be the fusion of the ancient three goddesses Anat, Astarte, and Asherah (Stuckey 2009a, 2). She was renowned all around the Mediterranean and beyond. We have found temples dedicated to her as far as Petra, linking her to the Venus goddess Al-Uzza and even in Britain by the end of the Roman Empire. Her cult was enduring until at least the seventh century CE. Sharing aspects of the three Mediterranean goddesses, trees and ponds were sacred to her. Men were known to castrate themselves for her, a practice that was later forbidden by the Christians. For the great Cybele and Magna Mater, males would also willingly sacrifice their physical masculinity to gain approval of these great figures. Just like the other lunar goddesses, she was a figure of transition and transformation. According to Lucian who visited her temple, Atargatis was equated to many goddesses but mostly Hera and Aphrodite Urania. At her temple in Hierapolis, a sacred lake contained special fishes: "There is too a lake in the same place, not far from the temple in which many sacred fishes of different kinds are reared. Some of these grow to a great size; they are called by names, and approach when called" (Lucian 1913, 81). Therefore, she bore magical properties related to the watery world.

It is those very complicated aspects that make Atargatis interesting and that brought her into the celestial cults of the moon and potentially of the Cygnus or Swan constellation. It is said that her association with the sea links her to the dawn.

NANSHE

The symbolism of the goose-swan was closely connected to the Sumerian goddess Nanshe, who was a goddess of justice and divination. Along with the healing temples that were present in the ancient world, the Nanshe temples were places where dreams could be interpreted. The priest or priestess was seen as a wisdom carrier, and premonitions could be divulged to the seeker. It is said that waterbirds were associated with this goddess. Sometimes they looked like a goose or a swan; the identification is not clear. These birds were associated with premonitions and the caring of family and citizens, which is suitable for a powerful goddess like Nanshe (Steinkeller 1994).

Of course, Nanshe and her functions were absorbed by Inanna eventually. Swans or geese are thought to also be features of the goddess Inanna and eventually of Hera and Aphrodite (Asher-Greve 2013). This is no trivial information because Aphrodite was depicted during Hellenistic times as riding a goose or a chariot drawn by swans. As scholar Margaret Merisante has noticed herself:

> Both of these sacred animals display complex symbolism and clear associations with goddesses. Aphrodite, Hera, Leda, Helen, Holda, Sarasvati, Solntse, Isis, Saul, Devi, and Tibetan dakinis are all linked to swans or geese. Furthermore, nearly every one of these goddesses are emblematic of sexuality, water, death, light, cycles or time, and new life. Additionally, the Cygnus or Swan constellation was viewed in ancient times as both a guide for the living and a psychopomp for the dead due to its position in the skies. Visually, Cygnus lies in the middle of the Milky Way, the river of stars, which has long been seen as both the source of life and the eternal residence of the dead. (Merisante 2015, 5)

Additionally, Merisante mentions that horses are also symbols of death, time, and light and reflect the movement of Venus, the sun, and the moon, as the original symbol of Astarte has shown us. Indeed, horses have always been incorporated with the realm of the dead and of dreams. We can then understand the significant symbolism that these goddesses bore and particularly how the spiritual link with the Cygnus constellation is important so that we can work better with these energies. The riding lady of the sea is a guide to the realm of the ancestors.

The Goddess and the Cygnus Constellation

During the Bronze Age on the island of Cyprus there were many amulets found in the shape of crosses. These were cruciform goddesses. Their arms extending like wings could possibly represent a bird-goddess, which was a prevalent motif on this island. It also has been interpreted as women dancing around, in a form of ritual dance (During 2023). Some figurines were also shown wearing a cross-like amulet. Even in North Africa, goddess Tanit was also sometimes depicted as wearing a cross, a figure that resembles the cruciform goddesses. I think that these crosses could be linked to the very ancient Cygnus constellation. Deneb

Ancient Cypriot goddess figurine, ca. 3000–2500 BCE (Getty Villa Museum)

is the brightest star in the Cygnus constellation and forms a cross in the sky called the northern cross and points directly to the Milky Way, the ancestral home of the souls.

It is very likely that myths and lore from Cygnus and Deneb were there even before the first scripts and other forms of writing appeared. I think it mostly survived as oral traditions and into the collective memory of humanity, like many other recurring symbols. As symbols of the dawn, transformation, luck, destiny, and rebirth, it is easy to see why these different goddesses were associated together. The numerous stories we still have about Cygnus come from folklore, including tales of the mother goose or the swan maidens who shape-shift between bird and human forms. Appearing as young women, they catch the eyes of young men who see them coming from the sky and bathing during the night. These tales of transformation with the act of shape-shifting and sorcery could symbolize the transformation of the souls, according to folkloristics (Hatto 1961). It seems like the swan was an important symbol in ancient times. In many Eurasian cultures, humans are thought to descend from a swan maiden ancestress (Hatto 1961). She might be linked to ancestral matrilineal descent in some cultures. As a strong symbolic bird, the swan roams the three spheres of the world—the heavens, the seas, and Earth. It is truly a celestial symbol.

The Cygnus constellation is best seen in the northern celestial hemisphere from June to December. It is known as the celestial cross, and during September the constellation can best be seen flying toward the west and appearing almost as a straight cross. Because the Summer Triangle is formed by our three most important stars, including Deneb from the Swan constellation, and is near the Milky Way, there is no doubt that this area of the night sky must have been an intriguing and spectacular sight for ancient people when they looked up. Although it moves across the sky, the cross of the Swan can be seen all year long.*

*"Cygnus Constellation," Constellation Guide website, 2024.

As author Gavin White has noted, the Greek literature about the Syrian goddesses is very explicit about bird references. For example, it was forbidden to eat doves and fish as they were sacred to the goddess (White 2014). Perhaps we find the origin of the swan in the fish and the dove. In ancient Mesopotamia these two were related, and the swallow was identified with fish. There is a strong association with birds and water, as water is healing and a life-giving force as well as a dangerous zone. Water was always held sacred and associated with goddesses in many cultures. Aphrodite is said to have been born from the egg of a swan as was the Syrian goddess who was born from an egg brought by two fish. Because the sea reflects the night sky, it was easy for the ancient mind to connect these two elements. By sending something into the waters, you may have a chance to reach the heavens.

These ancient spirits and energies are still very present with us, and if you feel called by the sea and astral powers, I encourage you to listen to them and to practice star magic more often to be more in tune with the ancestral goddesses. If you would like to visit a specific place to honor the Swan constellation and the Milky Way, it is possible to visit ancient sites such as Newgrange in Ireland.

SYMBOLIC MESSAGE
☙ *Transformation* ☙

The message from the lady of the sea is this one: You will face rebirth when you die and heal from your wounds. The great goddess of the sea gets her powers from desire. Desire is one of the strongest forces you can have in your life. Just like the moon and Venus, you can transform and arise as a new person. Observe what you have accomplished. How have you changed? What have you left that has transformed you? How do you manifest desire? The power of manifestation will give you what you want in life and transform it. Do not be afraid to let the duality of both masculine and feminine essences transform you. You cannot be truly yourself if you do not embrace both energies, just like the goddesses.

HOW TO WORK WITH

The Lady of the Sea

The stars and constellations related to the goddesses explored in this chapter are best seen from February to September. Spring marks the rise of Venus, and the Cygnus constellation is best seen during September. August is known to be an auspicious time to celebrate many goddesses, under the manifestation of Sirius or Venus. The best incense you can offer those deities is cypress and aromatic herbs.

These complex goddesses had multiple roles and symbols. The lady of the sea is a powerful healing energy, but she is also the best deity to ask for help when dealing with troubles in relationships and sexuality. Because these goddesses serve as guides to the land of the souls, it is recommended to start a devotion to your ancestors to honor the work of these deities. The best way to honor your ancestors is to set up a small altar in your home where you can offer a daily prayer or offering. Simply putting pictures of or objects from deceased people who were important to you will be beneficial for your ancestral work.

As for the granting of wishes and prosperity, the best time to ask is when the moon and Venus are in their evening phases during twilight. This is the period when the lady of the sea enters the underworld and transforms, and it is a good time to write down your desires and send them into waters. It is best to write these down on gold-colored tree leaves. Gold is the color of these goddesses, and using leaves will not pollute the waters. Ideally, if you do this during the night, make sure to find a water source that reflects the starry sky. When the stellar object enters the underworld, she disappears, and that is the time to think about your transformation and practice the rituals of death of self.

Dances are the best art form you can give to the celestial energy of the swan guide.

((O))

Egyptian mummy breast covering with the goddess Nut (Martin von Wagner Museum, Würzburg, Germany)

CELESTIAL HEALING

Rituals for Reconnecting
with the Stellar Goddesses

Every man and every woman is a star.

LIBER *AL VEL LEGIS,* I:3

Come forth, o children, under the stars, & take your fill of love!

LIBER *AL VEL LEGIS,* I:12

Now that we have gained a deeper understanding of the significance of ancient goddesses in the lives of our ancestors, how can we reconnect with this aspect in our own lives? Together, we have explored the profound presence and mystical nature of these goddesses in the celestial realm and the underworld. There is a way to reintegrate this ancient magic into our lives, but it requires us to reestablish a connection with the natural world, which we may have neglected. Take a stroll through the forest and listen to the whispers of the wind. Embrace a tree and see if you sense something extraordinary. Walk on the Earth barefoot and feel its energy. Tune in to the sacred sounds of a flowing spring or the crashing waves of the sea. Always remember that there is a harmonious song emanating from the energies of the environment we inhabit.

A good way to begin reconnecting with the cosmos is by dedicating yourself to a specific spirit or entity each day. This could be a saint, a familiar tree, or a nearby water source. By investing a small amount of energy into this daily dedication, you will establish a solid foundation for more profound magical practices. Express gratitude for your existence by offering a small tribute each day to your chosen spirit or entity. Consider burying these offerings in the soil to establish a connection with the underworld. Once you feel a sense of reconnection with yourself and your environment, take the opportunity to familiarize yourself with the celestial map of your location. Spend time observing sunrises and sunsets whenever possible. Study the night sky and pay attention to the movements of celestial objects. Explore and learn about the ones that most captivate you.

If you have already identified the aspect of the goddesses that resonates with you (creatrix, warrior, healer, or lady of the sea) or if a particular constellation calls to you, consider performing a small act of devotion to the goddess or constellation each night. This could take the form of a prayer, lighting a candle, engaging in meditation, making a drawing, composing a poem, or singing a song. Remember, every little dedication you make on a daily basis contributes to the development of a consistent and profound devotional practice. Over time, you will notice a transformation in your everyday life. You will sense that your desires, expressed through celestial magic, begin to manifest in various ways.

In this chapter, we focus on the ancient art of celestial healing as it was practiced in the ancient world. Once again, our major sources of knowledge for these practices come from around the Mediterranean and the Near Eastern worlds (Wee 2014). But similar practices do still exist today, in, for example, India—though it is now rarer because fewer have a relationship with the night sky.

It is thought that the ancient Near Eastern healers would bring their medicinal herbs and remedies outside at night positioned under a particular star so that the plants could absorb its power. The main constellation that was used for this purpose was Lyra because of its association with the healing goddess Gula, but there were other stars that could also be used for irradiation of herbal recipes. For example, we know that Orion was used for the potency of herbs and healing, particularly in Greco-Egyptian times, and Ursa Major was also a major one for spiritual healing and to help its followers. Venus, the sun, and the moon are major celestial influences in healing as well. But before we look up at the sky for its powers, let's see how it is possible to summon the divinities down into our lives.

MAKING THE GODDESS COME ALIVE

If we perceive deities as celestial forces and energetic emanations from nature, it follows that their presence could also be invoked into physical objects. In ancient times, gods and goddesses were initially represented by natural elements like wooden pillars and stones. As time passed, these representations evolved to become more anthropomorphic. Unfortunately, many of these wooden statues were lost over the years due to fires. Because the statues representing deities held such immense significance, they were often plundered during times of war. The destruction of temples and the theft of these divine figures became the subject of poetic literature known as lamentations.

Statues held great significance in ancient religions as they resided in the most sacred areas of temples. During grand festivals and celebrations, these statues would be taken out in processions and revered. Occasionally, the statues of gods would even be taken on visits to other cities. This tradition can still be observed in various parts of the world, including within the Catholic religion, where statues are paraded. In private worship as well, replicas of statues were kept in the homes of ordinary people to pay homage to specific deities.

Since the most revered deities were associated with celestial objects in the sky, various rituals involving natural elements, such as wood, were performed to invoke their power and magic. In order for prayers and devotion to be answered by the gods, their energy had to be summoned and embodied within the statues. This elaborate ritual was solely conducted for ceremonial purposes and served to bring forth the energy of the stars and allow a god or goddess to accompany the devotee on Earth.

Luckily, we have found preserved texts telling us how these rituals were performed. There are two versions of a ritual called *mîs-pî*, or "the washing of the mouth," which was performed in ancient Mesopotamia and surrounding cultures. This extremely long and complex ritual consisted of breathing life into a new effigy of a chosen deity, which was then set in a temple. In Egypt this ritual was called "the opening of the mouth."

I have drawn inspiration from the original text found on cuneiform tablets, but I present my own version of this ritual to make it more relatable for today's practitioner, replacing the original animal sacrifice with different offerings, which I have found works perfectly. If you like, you can perform this ritual daily to form a relationship to a star that speaks to you—or to a particular goddess or god. I have decided not to incorporate specific deity names but to link their planetary equivalents so that the ritual is not fixed exclusively on ancient Egyptian or Mesopotamian deities.

((O))
Breathing Life into a Deity

In the first part of the ritual, the mouth of the statue in which the induction was to take place was washed to clean and purify the statue of any human contamination. Sometimes washing of the ears was also performed to make sure the deity would be able to hear prayers and incantations from its followers. The next step was the opening of the mouth, during which the divine energy was breathed into the statue through its mouth. During this step, herbs, such as cypress or cedar, and oils, such as cedar oil or ghee, were used.

Before trying this ritual, there is some setup to do.

On Stones, Incense, Wood, and Libations

You first have to make a statue or representation of your chosen goddess. It could take the form of a traditional statue made of wood or stone, or you could just carve a symbol into wood or inscribe it in clay. Traditionally, when these rituals were written, anthropomorphic statues were used so they had a mouth to wash and breathe in.

The effigy of the deity was usually put in a reed hut to receive the radiation from the stars, but the figure can be positioned outdoors and does not need to be in a hut. Since the goddess is left outside overnight, this ritual is best performed in a private or secluded location. You also have to bring the statue near a body of water, if possible; otherwise you'll need an additional basin of water (three rather than the two called for in the list below). The water needs to be sanctified or made holy by setting it outside under the sun for one day.

The materials you will need to perform the washing of the mouth include:

2 basins filled with holy water
Statue of the goddess
Offerings (for instance, olive oil, fruits, poem, song, or dance)
Pillar candle to act as a torch
Bowl to hold the offerings
Beer
Milk
Wine
Honey or syrup
Cypress incense
Flower petals
Linen cloth
7 small cups
1 carnelian stone and 1 lapis lazuli stone
Cedar oil
Honey and ghee (clarified butter) mixed together

Initial Practice Steps: Sunset

1. To cleanse the mouth of a goddess, select an auspicious day and prepare two sacred water basins. (Auspicious days are considered lucky by the quality of their nature. They change every month. Vedic astrology websites can be a good resource for finding an auspicious day.)

2. Place the goddess effigy near a water source—river, pool, lake, sea, or small basin of holy water placed outside, ideally in a garden.

3. Wash the goddess's mouth (or surface if there is no face) three times with sanctified water from one of the basins and set up offerings for her (such as oil, beer, meal, wine, fruits, poem, etc.).

4. Raise your right hand and repeat the incantation "Born in heaven" three times.

5. In front of the goddess, recite the incantation "From today you go before the stars of heaven" three times.

6. Face the goddess toward the sunset. Hold her hand or touch the statue and recite the incantation "Come down from the sky" three times.

7. Light the pillar candle and place it in front of the goddess.

8. Address the Milky Way as "Mother of life" three times while pouring beer, milk, wine, and syrup as offerings into the bowl in front of the statue.

9. Perform mouth washing with the libations and repeat the incantation "She who comes, her mouth is washed" three times.

10. Disassemble the offering arrangement by extinguishing the candle and pouring the bowl's contents into the earth. Leave the statue and the basins overnight and return in the morning.

Procession from the Water into the Garden: Sunrise

1. At sunrise, carry the statue of the goddess from the water source to a nearby garden (or another outdoor location where you have access to flowers). Light the cypress incense.

2. Create a circle of petals in the garden and place the statue in the center on a linen cloth, facing the sunrise.

3. Offer beer to the holy waters in the basins as a libation. Raise your right hand and recite the incantation "Mirror of Orion, divine reflections" three times each in front of the two water basins.

4. Collect water from one of the two holy water basins, then pour it into seven small cups and arrange them around the goddess.

5. Place carnelian and lapis lazuli stones in the second holy water basin and let them rest there for at least fifteen minutes.

6. Remove the stones from the basin and place them in a mixture of cedar oil, honey, and ghee. Use the coated stones for mouth washing and recite "She who comes, her mouth is open" three times.

7. Disassemble the offering arrangement before sunset. Natural ingredients such as herbs, honey, flowers, etc., can be left outside; other materials should be returned to your home.

8. To complete the ritual, kneel before the effigy and recite three times: "Dear goddess, welcome."

With this effigy, you are ready to start a relationship with your chosen entity. In the days and weeks that follow, call upon the deity you have summoned and express gratitude for her presence. When the goddess has been invoked, she can reside in her sanctuary, in your home or a dedicated temple, and receive sustenance, clothing, cleansing, and prayers as long as she remains there. She is present to hear human prayers and safeguard the sanctuary she inhabits. At times, deities may depart. This was a cause of distress among ancient peoples. Many ancient poems lament the departure of gods and goddesses from cities under attack. When temples were destroyed, it signaled the deity's absence. In such cases, the ritual must be repeated.

PROTECTIVE SPIRIT FIGURINES

To add extra protection to your home or when you perform a ritual, you can also invoke celestial energies into little guardians. In ancient households, it was common for household members to have relationships with a large variety of spirits. Each person had a personal spirit and dedicated his or her practice to it, but the house also had spirits to protect it. Since the ancient mind gave importance to the night sky and its objects, people believed that the elemental energies of the seven main planets could be used as guardian spirits. In ancient Mesopotamia, these protective spirits were called *lamassu*.*

The following ritual, inspired by and adapted from a ritual explained in *Mesopotamian Protective Spirits: The Ritual Texts* by F. A. M. Wiggerman, was intended to protect a household with seven spirits that represented the

---

*Goddess Lama was initially a feminine protective spirit who would come before an incantation and had a function as Inanna's or Bau's messenger. Later in time this function was transformed into the Assyrian hybrid winged-bull Lamassu.

seven days of the week. The planetary influence for each day of the week is transferred into the figurines, and as such they act as protective amulets but also as messengers of the divine cosmos.

((○))
Invoking the Seven Spirits of Luck

Make seven figures with modeling clay. They can be very simple. If you have wood-carving skills, you can craft them from wood. These figures usually have tiaras on their heads, as a symbol of their celestial roles. Position each with the left hand on the chest and a stick in the right hand: this is a position of both protection and attack. They do not need to have facial features; their most important features are their colors. Each figurine will be painted a different color and will bear its name written on its back.

- The first figurine will be red and called "Day of Life," associated with Tuesday and the planet Mars.
- The second will be white, known as "Day of Plenty," linked to the Moon and Monday.
- The third will be gray, known as "Day of Splendor," corresponding to Venus and Friday.
- The fourth will be black, known as "Good Day." associated with Saturn and Saturday.
- The fifth will be yellow, known as "Fair-Faced Day," linked to Jupiter and Thursday.
- The sixth will be blue, known as "Righteous Day," corresponding to Mercury and Wednesday.
- The seventh will be orange, known as "Day That Brings Life," associated with the Sun and Sunday.

Once you have made the figures, go outside to consecrate them. You will need the following for the ritual:

Offerings: a small cake, dates, and beer
Small table

Water in a small container

Juniper incense

Ideally, you perform the ritual in the woods. If you don't have any woods nearby, try your backyard or garden or a park. If practical, make a small ritual fire; otherwise, light a candle. This ritual should be done at sunrise.

1. Once you find a suitable setting, place the figures so they are facing east, toward the rising sun.
2. Set up the small table and place the offerings on it; sweep around the table.
3. Kneel before the figurines and light the incense. Consecrate them with water and incense by sprinkling them with water and waving the incense smoke over them. To consecrate with fire, use a candle to trace a small circle in the air in front of the figurine.
4. While you and the figures face the sun, recite:

Great sun, the one who cares for all heaven and Earth.
  You are the one who guides the living and the dead.
  Replenished in your divinity, the consecrated statues
  that will stand in the house of [state your name] will
  throw back all evil. You are the statues that repel all
  evil. The ones that came from heaven and who are
  strong. You shine your powers through the radiance
  that was endowed upon you.
Guard your right and your left, may you never fail at
  watching.
May the evil of malignant energies not approach me or
  my house.

Keep these little guardians in your house, positioned near windows and doorways. Any liminal spaces should be protected to keep bad energies from entering your home. This custom is as old as humanity, and many cultures had specific rituals and objects to protect their homes, especially at night.

INVOKING THE CREATRIX

The following rituals are inspired from ancient astral rituals that were performed to obtain the powers of specific stellar objects. As we have explored, the creatrix is a complex divinity who has the power of the underworld sun but also that of the Milky Way and the starry night sky. The sacredness of the divine powers was intrinsically connected to the land. When you visit the Mediterranean world, you understand how the landscape reflects the divine world that is above and below.

To start these rituals, which you can use to connect with the goddesses, I have provided Orphic hymns for each of the goddess archetypes: creatrix, warrior, healer, and lady of the sea. The Orphic hymns originate in Orphism, a mystery cult that promised a better afterlife and was inspired by the underworld journey of Orpheus. We do not know much about this cult since it was secretive, but we have many poems and hymns giving the Orphic worldview and how the cult revered all of the cosmos and nature. We do know that, as early as the sixth century BCE, the cult forbade animal sacrifice, and followers refused to eat anything that came from animals, including eggs, for fear that their spirits would haunt them. It was believed that the suffering of animals would make humans sick.

To offer this hymn to the creatrix, it is accompanied by burning aromatic substances, such as frankincense and myrrh.

> Mother of Gods [Meter Theon], great nurse of all, draw
>   near, divinely honor'd, and regard my pray'r:
> Thron'd on a car, by lions drawn along, by bull-destroying
>   lions, swift and strong,
> Thou sway'st the sceptre of the pole divine, and the world's
>   middle seat, much-fam'd, is thine.
> Hence earth is thine, and needy mortals share their
>   constant food, from thy protecting care:
> From thee at first both Gods and men arose; from thee, the
>   sea and ev'ry river flows.
> Vesta [Hestia], and source of good, thy name we find to
>   mortal men rejoicing to be kind;

For ev'ry good to give, thy soul delights; come, mighty
    pow'r, propitious to our rites,
All-taming, blessed, Phrygian saviour, come, Saturn's
    [Kronos's] great queen, rejoicing in the drum. Celestial,
    ancient, life-supporting maid, fanatic Goddess, give thy
    suppliant aid;
With joyful aspect on our incense shine, and, pleas'd,
    accept the sacrifice divine.*

You can use this hymn before any ritual to dedicate your practice to this particular energy.

CELESTIAL IRRADIATION

In the ancient Sumerian world, one aspect of medicine was to put the patient under the night sky in an open temple to let the stars irradiate energies toward the disease. Some similar practices were found in Greece as well, with the temples of Asclepius. In the Asklepion, the healing process was held in the temple, and people would dream about the god that would come and heal them; this practice was called dream incubation. Although celestial irradiation is a little bit different, both practices seemed to have worked well. The setup for celestial bathing is quite simple. Although in ancient times everything was more elaborate, I have simplified the ritual so that it works better in today's world.

☾○☽
Sleeping under the Stars

You can do this in your garden or backyard; if you have access to a space in the wilderness, that would be even better. Most ancient people were healed while resting in small reed huts that were opened at night. Today, we can lie inside a tent or lie directly outside on a mat. For this practice, you will need the following.

---

*Orphic Hymns, "XXVI. To the Mother of the Gods," translated by Thomas Taylor (1792), Theoi Classical Texts Library website.

- Guardian spirits: Here you can use the protective figurines you made in the previous ritual.
- Sesame oil: Still used in Ayurveda, an ancient traditional Indian medicine, sesame oil has been used for millennia in every culture. Known for its healing and soothing effect, this anti-inflammatory oil can be applied all over the skin and should also be left as an offering in this ritual.
- Lotus perfume oil: Although this oil is not essential, if you can procure it, I highly recommend it. The ancient Egyptians thought that lotus oil was a healing divinity. The lotus flower is known to rejuvenate and help the skin breathe. It is also a good anti-inflammatory.
- Wine libation in a cup: This wine is meant to spend the night under the night sky with you. You will drink it just before sunrise and leave a little as an offering.

This night ritual starts at dusk and ends at dawn.

1. Address the sun at dusk with a personal prayer. As the night gets darker, address Ursa Major and ask for the healing you are looking for. These two prayers can be done standing up with arms raised. The palms of your hands should be facing the sky. This was known as an efficient protective position in the ancient world. In Christianity it is referred to the orans posture.

2. For the rest of the night, you can sleep under the night sky, accompanied by your protective spirits. As mentioned previously, you can be in a tent with the flap open, especially if the sky is clear. I recommend that you meditate on your health and visualize what you would like to see happening in your body or mind. In this meditation stage, apply oil (sesame or lotus or both) to your body and leave some outside as an offering. Let yourself go to sleep.

3. Try to wake before the sun rises, and when the sun appears, once again thank the sun, the moon, Ursa Major, and especially the constellation Lyra for its energy given during the night. Thank them for their presence and healing aid.

4. End the ritual with another meditation. See yourself getting better,

feeling better. Drink most of the wine, give the rest to the Earth. Be grateful.

You can repeat this night ritual as often as you see fit.

INVOKING THE WARRIOR

The following ritual was inspired by ancient rites for protection that can be linked with the figure of the warrior. We start with the Orphic hymn to Nike (Victory). To invoke this one, you will need to burn frankincense resin.

> O Powerful Victory [Nike], by men desir'd, with adverse
>   breasts to dreadful fury fir'd,
> Thee I invoke, whose might alone can quell contending
>   rage, and molestation fell:
> 'Tis thine in battle to confer the crown, the victor's prize,
>   the mark of sweet renown;
> For thou rul'st all things, Victory [Nike] divine! And glorious
>   strife, and joyful shouts are thine.
> Come, mighty Goddess, and thy suppliant bless, with
>   sparkling eye, elated with success;
> May deeds illustrious thy protection claim, and find, led on
>   by thee immortal Fame. *

If you wish to call for success and victory in your deeds or help with anxiety, you can use this hymn before performing a ritual with the energy of the warrior.

ASTRAL BATHING FOR SPIRITUAL HELP

As mentioned, medicine and magical healing were intrinsically linked. Healing practices were used for physical ailments and for mental ones too. Some mental illnesses were often linked to a curse sent by the gods

---

*Orphic Hymns, "XXXII. To Victory," translated by Thomas Taylor (1792), Theoi Classical Texts Library website.

to someone. Sometimes it was also thought that some unlucky people were struck with specific demons that would cause them to be anxious or depressed. Mental well-being was seen as something mysterious but worthy of help. For example, the goddess Hygieia, or sometimes called Athena Hygieia, would help with mental illness in ancient Greece. As such, spiritual help and blessings can be requested from the warrior goddesses.

《○》
Invoking a Blessing

This celestial ritual is similar to celestial bathing but with a different goal to achieve. This one has prayers and actions aimed to help soothe the mind. It should be performed on the fifteenth day of the month, when the sun and the moon meet at dawn. You will need the following.

> Clean clothes
> Juniper incense
> Beer
> Cypress incense
> Cow's milk

1. Spend the night under the sky, in a tent if desired. Let the stars of the night irradiate you while you sleep.
2. Wake just before dawn and change your clothes. In ancient times, the irradiation of celestial bodies on clothes, objects, or a person was thought to sometimes be affected by malevolent energies. Hence, before and after a ritual, it was believed that changing clothes would mark yourself as a new person.
3. While the sun is rising, sit facing the north.
4. With both your hands, offer juniper incense to the sun and a libation of beer.
5. Offer cypress incense to the moon and a libation of milk while you recite this prayer:

May this be a body of joy.

May you give benediction to this body that I Inhabit and
benedict the owner of this house.

6. When you have said this in front of the sun and imagining the Eagle
star, you shall speak as follows:

Grant me eternal sunshine and boundless joy, allowing
me to live a long and fulfilling life.
May I delight in the home I have constructed, experiencing
daily happiness and jubilation within its walls.
May I successfully attain all that I strive for.
Send forth the celestial messengers to bless my endeavors.
I humbly implore you to listen to my plea, so that I may
offer praises in your name.

7. Let the offerings for the deities remain outside as you sit and breathe
watching the sun rise. Envision yourself being happy and healthy.

INVOKING THE HEALER

The healer, goddess of darkness and keeper of powerful stars and
constellations, is an easy energy to just soak in at night. You can benefit
from celestial irradiation without having to perform a complex ritual. We
have explored how the goddesses of death and night were often related to
healing powers. As such, we invoke the healer with the Orphic hymn to
Nyx or Night. Before reciting this invocation, you should burn a variety of
herbs as an offering.

Night [Nyx], parent goddess, source of sweet repose,
from whom at first both Gods and men arose, Hear,
blessed Venus [Kypris], deck'd with starry light, in
sleep's deep silence dwelling Ebon night! Dreams
and soft case attend thy dusky train, pleas'd with the
length'ned gloom and fearful strain. Dissolving anxious
care, the friend of Mirth, with darkling coursers
riding round the earth. Goddess of phantoms and

of shadowy play, whose drowsy pow'r divides the
nat'ral day: By Fate's decree you constant send the
light to deepest hell, remote from mortal sight. For dire
Necessity which nought withstands, invests the world
with adamantine bands.

Be present, Goddess, to thy suppliant's pray'r, desir'd by all,
whom all alike revere,

Blessed, benevolent, with friendly aid dispell the fears of
Twilight's dreadful shade. *

As with the other rituals, you can open any of your work for healing and divination with this hymn dedicated to the night sky.

HEALING RITUALS WITH THE STARRY NIGHT

This ritual is inspired by Hittite pit rituals, during which holes were dug and offerings were put into the ground to receive both celestial and Earth energies. It was believed that putting objects inside these holes for an entire night would imbue them with healing powers and good luck.

☾○☽
Healing Incantation

This ritual is a simple incantation to help in any healing process.

1. Dig a small hole in the ground in your garden or in a park.
2. Stand under the night sky and recite the following:

I Stand here today before Night. I humbly request your
judgment and decision regarding my situation. I ask
you to remove any negativity from my body and being.
Please entrust these negative aspects to the counselor of
the netherworld, under the watchful eye of the overseer.

---

*Orphic Hymns, "II. To Night," translated by Thomas Taylor (1792), Theoi Classical Texts Library website.

*Let the chief gatekeeper of the netherworld securely seal
    the gate behind them.*

*Take away these negative elements and send them to the
    land of no return.*

*As your devoted servant, I seek a life of good health
    and well-being.*

*Cleanse me from all negativities using your divine
    power, so that I may offer pure water as a tribute to
    honor you.*

*Restore my well-being, allowing me to joyfully sing your
    praises.*

3. Pour water into the ground after you recite this.
4. Write what you wish to heal or get rid of on a paper and put it in
   the water in the ground.
5. Leave an offering, such as cake. Ancient priestesses used to bake
   cakes for goddesses related to the night and the sky. Artemis, for
   example, received crescent moon cakes. Queens of the heavens
   such as Asherah and Astarte are thought to have received ash
   cakes made with raisins. You can find a reference to cakes being
   baked for the Queen of Heaven in the Bible in Jeremiah 7 and 44.

INVOKING THE LADY OF THE SEA

As we explored together, the lady of the sea was a powerful figure that
could be responsible for dreams, divination, powerful protection, and
erotic fulfillment. Eros and Thanatos, or desire and death, are often linked
together as the forces that keep us alive. Without the sexual libido and the
thriving desire to live, we would not be able to sustain our lives in the
short time we are here on Earth. I have chosen here to call upon the lady
of the sea with the Orphic hymn to the moon. You should burn aromatic
herbs as an offering and recite the following:

*Hear, Goddess queen, diffusing silver light, bull-horn'd
    and wand'ring thro' the gloom of Night. With stars*

*surrounded, and with circuit wide Night's torch
extending, thro' the heav'ns you ride: Female and
Male with borrow'd rays you shine, and now full-
orb'd, now tending to decline. Mother of ages, fruit-
producing Moon [Mene], whose amber orb makes
Night's reflected noon: Lover of horses, splendid,
queen of Night, all-seeing pow'r bedeck'd with starry
light. Lover of vigilance, the foe of strife, in peace
rejoicing, and a prudent life:*

*Fair lamp of Night, its ornament and friend, who giv'st
to Nature's works their destin'd end.*

*Queen of the stars, all-wife Diana hail! Deck'd with a
graceful robe and shining veil;*

*Come, blessed Goddess, prudent, starry, bright, come
moony-lamp with chaste and splendid light, Shine on
these sacred rites with prosp'rous rays, and pleas'd
accept thy suppliant's mystic praise.**

((O))

Purification and Protection for the Home

This ritual was used to bring protection into the home by summoning the energies of the stars to the ground. It is best performed near a river or lake. You will need the following.

> Dagger
> Small goddess figurine
> Vegetable oil
> Beer in a small cup
> Mead in a small cup
> Meal in a small cup
> Hand towel

---

*Orphic Hymns, "VIII. To the Moon," translated by Thomas Taylor (1792), Theoi Classical Texts Library website.

1. Dig a small pit with the dagger and put the figurine into the pit.
2. Recite:

> *Dear beloved goddess, I, a humble human came to seek*
> *your help.*
> *Hear my plea so that I can partake of your protection.*

3. Pour the liquid offerings (oil, beer, mead) and the meal into the hole and cover with the hand towel.
4. Recite:

> *O pit, take the offering of purification.*
> *Examine the offerings and bring forth purification and*
> *luck so I can take it into my home.*

5. Your hand towel will now be imbued with the energies of the ground. Bring it home where it will have a protecting effect.

I suspect that this ritual has survived through the European custom of putting a scarf outside on the night of February 1 to bring purification and healing properties to it from the goddess Brigit.

INVOKING THE QUEENS OF THE HEAVENS

The final ritual is based upon the three stars that make up the Summer Triangle—Vega, Altair, and Deneb—the sacred triangle of the summer sky. The ancient goddesses we explored in this book are all personifications of death and rebirth but their key role is bringer of souls to the underworld. The devotion and cults dedicated to these goddesses were meant to protect one's life before the uncertainty of death. These rituals are difficult to find as they were mostly concealed in secret societies, called the mysteries. During the mysteries, devotees experienced a symbolic death and rebirth so that they would cease to fear death. In the caverns where the initiations took place, devotees would experience the darkness and nothingness of death and meet with the goddesses. The goddesses we explored often had places of worship in caverns, holes, and wells, hidden from the plain sight. The ancients believed that the powers of the stars were reflected through the waters or by drawing down the stars into the stones and lakes.

((○))
Making Peace with Death

There are two ways to connect with this powerful trio of fate: you can experience a dark ritual outside under the night sky or by going inside an enclosed space. As you now know, these three important stars are related to the healer, the lady of the sea, and the warrior. You can choose specific goddess names according to their function as well.

1. Dress in white, and when it is the darkest point of the night (around midnight), look up at the three stars—Vega, Altair, and Deneb— with your chest open and arms resting at your sides for a few minutes.

2. Prepare *Centaurea* flowers (knapweed)—using fresh flowers, if possible—and burn them in a fire. This plant is believed to facilitate communication with the stars.

3. Lift your two arms toward the sky and recite the following Orphic hymn to the stars:

> With holy voice I call the stars on high, pure sacred
>   lights and genii of the sky.
> Celestial stars, the progeny of Night, in whirling circles
>   beaming far your light,
> Refulgent rays around the heav'ns ye throw, eternal fires,
>   the source of all below.
> With flames significant of Fate ye shine, and aptly rule
>   for men a path divine.
> In seven bright zones ye run with wand'ring flames, and
>   heaven and earth compose your lucid frames:
> With course unwearied, pure and fiery bright forever
>   shining thro' the veil of Night.
> Hail twinkling, joyful, ever wakeful fires! Propitious shine
>   on all my just desires;

*These sacred rites regard with conscious rays, and end
    our works devoted to your praise**

4. Sit down and recite the following one time in three directions—
   north, east, and west:

   *Great maidens, great queens of the heavens
   I call for your protection and your wings to bless me
   May you bring peace in the adversity of death
   May you grant me a healthy life so that I may join you
       in old age.*

5. Meditate in the dark of your hidden space. Visualize the goddesses
   coming to you in their winged forms and taking you to the stars.
6. Try to sleep. You may or may not receive their visit in a dream.
7. When you wake up, light a candle and recite this last verse:

   *I have traveled to the land of the souls and back,
   I am now reborn within the sacred flame of life
   I have health and a long life ahead of me
   May I sing you and praise your names.*

8. Leave an offering in the space where you performed the ritual.

As you have now performed a ritual dedicated to the queens of the
heavens, take note of how you feel and how your life improves. This can
be repeated as often as you want.

---

*Orphic Hymns, "VI. To the Stars," translated by Thomas Taylor (1792), Theoi Classical
Texts Library website.

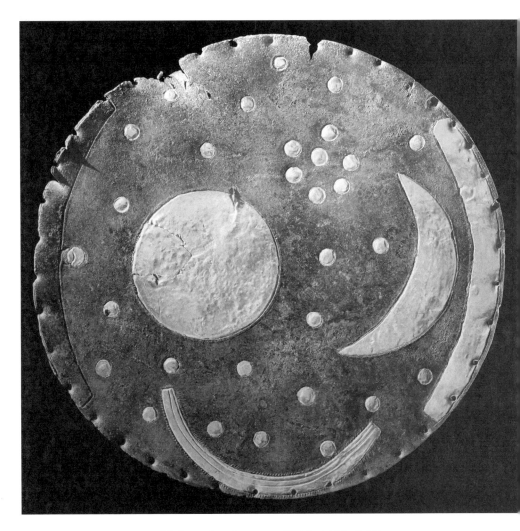

Nebra sky disc, ca. 1800–1600 BCE

Photo by Frank Vincentz

Our Legacy of Ancient Celestial Magic

I have presented in this book different practices spanning millennia and shown how these practices can help us to understand how ancient humans, though from very different cultures, perceived the world similarly through time. Many of the ancient celestial gods and goddesses and their rituals stem from the ancient Near East, which is the area I have mostly studied. Even if the periods after the Iron Age were not the focus of my research, there are many reasons to believe that this ancient Near Eastern knowledge and cosmology did survive at the end of antiquity through the Neoplatonic and Orphic schools, for example.

By the second century BCE, the celestial land of the deceased, often called hell, was an established belief. It was believed that this infernal land was located in the sublunar world. The belief that souls are related to the planets, even though it was an archaic belief, was becoming increasingly popular and largely influenced all gnostic systems later in time (Culianu 1979). This would lead to the development of many magical occult practices over the next centuries.

In this book, far from being perfect, I have presented powerful ancient figures and rituals that were significant for the people who lived in ancient times, people who were, indirectly, our ancestors. These ancient goddesses remain present in today's cultures, and some are even revered again today. Their celestial nature is not always understood, and I hope that I have presented a good overview of how ancient heavenly powers were spiritually significant and caring. I tried to remind us humans where we come from and where we go in the end. The connection with the very real nature we live in has been severed, and I have intended modestly, with this book, to help seekers reconnect with the cosmos. I hope I have been able to present the importance of the heavens, the seas, and the Earth and their interrelation with the different spheres of human lives. The subtle nature of ancient goddesses was not easy to present, as ancient religions were quite complicated and fluid. Because these goddesses were connected to many different aspects of stars, planets, and constellations, it was even more complicated to understand how these different energies affected the roles of these ancient figures. As such, there are still many secrets to uncover.*

We have explored how some ancient goddesses of the underworld were linked to the solar symbol, reinstating their roles as protective motherly figures. The sun as a female source worked in perfect balance with the masculine sun. The male solar aspect was responsible for deeds during the day and for judging people, while the sun goddess was the protectress of the dead and leader of the ancestors. Another solar figure related to death and war was the figure of the warrior maiden with the eagle as a symbol of justice and protective magic. Regarded as a highly powerful figure, the kings were fond of her protection. She became a symbol of state governance. We then explored the very ancient healing goddess under the magic of the star Vega and the moon and her symbolism as a goddess of the night. Potent spiritual awakening was linked to her magic. She could harness the powers to send vengeance as well. Finally, we explored the lunar aspect of the dual-gendered goddess and possibly swan maiden who

---

*Many goddesses or female spirits were also linked to tree worship, water worship, or cavern worship. These specific aspects of ancient goddess and spirit cults also need separate work and investigation.

took care of the deceased as well but who was also a strong force of desire and self-love. Adored by the common people, she was a figure of ancestral knowledge and a leader of the deceased, bringing them to the land of the eternal souls.

This ancient planetary or celestial magic has managed to survive through time to the present day. This is in part thanks to the city of Harran in Turkey, which stayed true to the ancient religions until the twelfth century CE. The people of Harran, who were called Sabians, continued to venerate the planets and stars even through the rise of Islam, and their ancient temples and star knowledge survived well into the Middle Ages. Medieval Arabian magic also valued this ancestral knowledge about the stars. As such, works like the *Picatrix* remained an important magic book that is useful for our understanding of ancient star magic. One of the most notorious temples in the city of Harran was that of Sin, the moon god who had a cult, along with diverse manifestations of Inanna well until the Middle Ages. This is quite unique because it gave rise to different spiritualities that also continued to work with celestial energies. The medieval and Renaissance magical grimoires of seals and invocations, for example, are just one of the many legacies of the ancient world of astral magic.

I hope that the ancient goddesses of the celestial realm, the queens of the heavens, continue to support us in our transition toward a new way to interact with the world and its creatures, and I hope they will forgive humanity for somehow forgetting that not everything is centered around male energy. This imbalance, I think, is coming to an end. While I continue researching the ancient art of working with the stars, I hope the voice of the goddess that told me to teach her true nature will be somewhat pleased, and I hope to be able to bring another work to life in the future.

BIBLIOGRAPHY

Abusch, Tzvi I. 1987. *Babylonian Witchcraft Literature.* Providence, RI: Brown Judaic Studies.

Albani, Matthias. 2004. "The Downfall of Helel, the Son of Dawn: Aspects of Royal Ideology in Isa 14:12–13." In *The Fall of the Angels,* edited by Christoph Auffarth and Loren T. Stuckenbruck, 62–86. Leiden, Netherlands: Brill.

Apuleius, Lucius. 1927. *Golden Ass: Being the Metamorphoses of Lucius Apuleius.* Translated by William Adlington. New York: Horace Liveright. First published 1566.

Aruz, Joan, Sarah B. Graff, and Yelena Rakic, eds. 2013. *Cultures in Contact: From Mesopotamia to the Mediterranean in the Second Millennium B.C.* New York: Metropolitan Museum of Art.

Asher-Greve, Julia M. 2013. *Goddesses in Context: On Divine Powers, Roles, Relationships and Gender in Mesopotamian Textual and Visual Sources.* Fribourg, Switzerland: Academic Press Fribourg.

Bachvarova, Mary. 2010. "Hecate: An Anatolian Sun-Goddess of the Underworld." SSRN Electronic Journal.

Barton, Tamysn. 1994. *Ancient Astrology.* Oxfordshire, UK: Routledge.

Beal, Richard H. 2002. "Dividing a God." In *Religions in the Graeco-Roman World,* edited by R. Van Den Broek, H. J. W. Drijvers, and H. S. Versnel, 197–208. Vol. 141 in *Magic and Ritual in the Ancient World* edited by Paul Mirecki and Marvin Meyer. Leiden, Netherlands: Brill.

Beaulieu A., and R. Mouterde. 1947. "La grotte d'Astarté à Wasta." In *Mélanges de l'Université Saint-Joseph*, tome 27, 1–20.

Benko, Stephen. 2004. *The Virgin Goddess: Studies in the Pagan and Christian Roots of Mariology*. Leiden, Netherlands: Brill.

Billing, Nils. 2004. "Writing an Image–The Formulation of the Tree Goddess Motif in the Book of the Dead, Ch. 59." *Studien Zur Altägyptischen Kultur* 32: 35–50.

Black, Jeremy, and Anthony Green. 1992. *Gods, Demons and Symbols of Ancient Mesopotamia: An Illustrated Dictionary*. London: British Museum Press.

Black, J. A., G. Cunningham, J. Ebeling, E. Flückiger-Hawker, E. Robson, J. Taylor, and G. Zolyomi. 1998–2006. *The Electronic Text Corpus of Sumerian Literature*. Faculty of Oriental Studies, University of Oxford.

Bonnet, Corinne, Thomas Galoppin, Eloide Guillon, Max Luaces, Asuman Lätzer-Lasar, Sylvain Lebreton, Fabio Porzia, Jörg Rüpke, and Emiliano Rubens Urciuoli. 2022. *Naming and Mapping the Gods in the Ancient Mediterranean: Spaces, Mobilities, Imaginaries*. Berlin: De Gruyter.

Bouillon, Hélène. 2014. "A New Perspective on So-Called Hathoric Curls." *Egypt and the Levant: International Journal for Egyptain Archaeology and Related Disciplines* 24: 209–26.

Breniquet, Catherine. 2002. "Animals in Mesopotamian Art." In *A History of the Animal World in the Ancient Near East*, edited by Billie Jean Collins, 145–68. Leiden, Netherlands: Brill.

Budin, Stephanie L. 2004. "A Reconsideration of the Aphrodite-Ashtart Syncretism." *Numen* 51 (2): 95–145.

———. 2014. "Before Kypris Was Aphrodite." In *Transformation of a Goddess*, edited by David T. Sugimoto. Fribourg, Switzerland: Academic Press Fribourg.

———. 2015. "Sexuality: Ancient Near East (except Egypt)." In *International Encyclopedia of Human Sexuality*, edited by A. Bolin and P. Whelehan. Hoboken, NJ: Wiley-Blackwell.

Cabrera, Rodrigo. 2018. "The Three Faces of Inanna: An Approach to her Polysemic Figure in Her Descent to the Netherworld." *Journal of Northwest Semitic Languages* 44: 41–79.

Cazelles, Henri. 1956. "L'Hymne Ugaritique a Anat." In *Syria: Revue d'Art Oriental et d'Archéologie*, vol. 33, edited by M. Rene Dussaud, 49–57. Paris: Librarie Orientaliste Paul Geuthner.

Chatzivasiliou, Despina. 2019. *Retour sur l'arkteia: lieux de culte et pratiques rituelles en Attique In: Dossier. Corps antiques: morceaux choisis.* Paris-Athènes: Éditions de l'École des hautes études en sciences sociales.

Collins, Billie Jean. 2014. "Necromancy, Fertility and the Dark Earth: The Use of Ritual Pits in Hittite Cult." In *Magic and Ritual in the Ancient World*, edited by Marvin W. Meyer and Paul Allan Mirecki. Leiden, Netherlands: Brill.

Cooper, Arabella. 2016. "The Eyes Have It: An In-Depth Study of the Tell Brak Eye Idols in the 4th Millennium BCE, with a Primary Focus on Function and Meaning." Honors thesis, University of Sydney.

Cornelius, Izak. 2008. *The Many Faces of the Goddess: The Iconography of the Syro-Palestinian Goddesses Anat, Astarte, Qedeshet, and Asherah c. 1500–1000 BCE.* Fribourg, Switzerland / Göttingen, Germany: Academic Press / Vandenhoeck & Ruprecht.

Culianu, Ioan P. 1979. "Démonisaion du cosmos et dualisme gnostique." *Revue de l'histoire des religions* 196 (1): 3–40

Czachesz, István. 2021. "Approaches to Ancient Religions." *Oxford Research Encyclopedia of Religion.*

Darnell, John Coleman. 1997. "The Apotropaic Goddess in the Eye." *Studien Zur Altägyptischen Kultur* 24: 35–48.

Day, John. 1986. "Asherah in the Hebrew Bible and Northwest Semitic Literature." *Journal of Biblical Literature* 105 (3): 385–408.

Descola, Philippe. 2005. *Par-delà Nature et Culture.* Paris: Gallimard.

———. 2020. "La nature, ca n'existe pas." Reporterre: Le média de l'écologie.

Draper, Eilish. 2020. "The Prophet, the Mother, the Avenger: An Examination of Gaia's Cult Worship and the 'Bricolage' in Her Myth." Thesis, Open Access Te Herenga Waka-Victoria University of Wellington.

Durand, Gilbert. 2016. *Les structures anthropologiques de l'imaginaire. Introduction à l'archétypologie générale.* Malakoff: Dunod, 2016

During, Bleda. 2023. "Reconsidering Cruciform Figurines of Chalcolithic Cyprus." In *Style and Society in the Prehistory of West Asia: Essays in Honour of Olivier P. Niewenhuyse* by B. S. Düring and P. M. M. G. Akkermans. Leiden, Netherlands: Sidestone Press. 149–56.

Edrey, Meir. 2008. "The Dog Burials at Achaemenid Ashkelon Revisited." *Journal of the Institute of Archaeology* of Tel Aviv University 35: 267–82.

Eliade, Mircea. 1971. *The Myth of the Eternal Return.* Princeton, NJ: Princeton University Press.

Falkenstein, Adam. 1953. "Sumerische Hymnen und Gebete." In *Sumerische und akkadische Hymnen und Gebete,* edited by Adam Falkenstein and Wolfram von Soden, 67–68. Zürich/Stuttgart: Artemis.

Faraone, Christopher A. 2014. "Inscribed Greek Thunderstones as House- and Body-Amulets in Roman Imperial Times." *Kernos* 27: 257–84.

Farrington, Oliver C. 1900. "The Worship and Folk-Lore of Meteorites." *Journal of American Folklore* 13 (50): 199–208.

Flaccus, Valerius. 1972. *Argonautica.* Books 1–8. Translated by John H. Mozley. Cambridge, MA: Harvard University Press.

Galili, Ehud, Liora Kolska-Horwitz, and Baruch Rosen. 2015. "Newe Yam: Anthropomorphic Figurine." Hadashot Arkheologiyot: Excavations and Survey in Israel.

Gimbutas, Marija. 1989. *The Language of the Goddess: Unearthing the Hidden Symbols of Western Civilization.* Foreword by Joseph Campbell. New York: Harper and Row.

Graves-Brown, Carolyn. 2010. *Dancing for Hathor: Women in Ancient Egypt.* London: Continuum.

Håland, Evy. 2012. "The Ritual Year of Athena: The Agricultural Cycle of the Olive, Girls' Rites of Passage, and Official Ideology." *Journal of Religious History* 36 (2).

Haliburton, R. G. 1920. "The Festival of the Dead." *Journal of the Royal Astronomical Society of Canada* 14: 292.

Hatto, A. T. 1961. "The Swan Maiden: A Folk-Tale of North Eurasian Origin?" *Bulletin of the School of Oriental and African Studies* 24 (2): 326–52.

Holden, Edward S. 1876. "The Horseshoe Nebula in Sagittarius." *Popular Science* 8: 269–81.

Hollman, J. C. 2007. "'The Sky's Things': |xam Bushman 'Astrological Mythology' as Recorded in the Bleek and Lloyd Manuscripts." *African Skies/Cieux Africains* 11: 8–11.

Homerin, T. E. 1985. "Echoes of a Thirsty Owl: Death and Afterlife in Pre-Islamic Arabic Poetry." *Journal of Near Eastern Studies* 44 (3): 165.

Horstmanshoff, H. J. F., and M. Stol, eds. 2004. *Magic and Rationality in Ancient Near Eastern and Graeco-Roman Medicine.* Volume 27 in *Studies in Ancient Medicine,* edited by Philip J. van der Eijk. Leiden, Netherlands: Brill.

Hutton, Ronald. 2021. *The Triumph of the Moon: A History of Modern Pagan Witchcraft.* Oxford, UK: Oxford University Press.

———. 2022. *Queens of the Wild: Pagan Goddesses in Christian Europe: An Investigation.* New Haven, CT: Yale University Press.

ibn-Al-Kalbi, Hisham. 1952. *The Book of Idols: Being a Translation from the Arabic of the Kitab Al-Asnam.* Translated by Nabih Amin Faris. Published online February 26, 2018.

Johnston, Sarah Iles, ed. 2007. *Ancient Religions.* Cambridge, MA: Harvard University Press.

Kajkowski, Kamil. 2015. "The Dog in Pagan Beliefs of Early Medieval North-Western Slavs." *Analecta Archaeologica Ressoviensia* 10: 199–240.

Karageorghis, Jacque. 1977. *La Grande Deesse de Chypre et son Culte. A Travers l'Iconographie de l'Epoque Neolithique au Vieme S.* Lyon, France: MOM Éditions.

Karageorghis, Vassos. 2003. "The Cult of Astarte in Cyprus." In *Symbiosis, Symbolism, and the Power of the Past: Canaan, Ancient Israel, and Their Neighbors, from the Late Bronze Age through Roman Palaestina,* edited by William G. Dever and Seymour Gitin, 215–22. University Park: Penn State University Press.

Kasak, Enn, and Raul Veede. 2001. "Understanding Planets in Ancient Mesopotamia." *Folklore* 16.

Konstantopoulos, Gina. 2015. "They Are Seven: Demons and Monsters in the Mesopotamian Textual and Artistic Tradition." Thesis, University of Michigan.

Krüger, Peter. 2012. "Nár: The Dead Man; The 'Lost' Constellation." Germanic Astronomy website.

Kurtik, G. E. 2019. "^{mul}uz3, $^{mul\ d}$Gula, and the Early History of Mesopotamian Constellations." *Journal for the History of Astronomy,* 50 (3): 339–59.

Lenzi, Adam. 2011. *Reading Akkadian Prayers and Hymns: An Introduction.* Atlanta, GA: Society of Biblical Literature.

Létourneau, Anne. 2022. "Tisser Pour Ashérah. La Participation Textile des Femmes au Culte en 2 R 23,7." *Mélanges de Sciences Religieuses* 78 (5): 60–71.

Lewis, Theodore J. 2011. "Athtartu's Incantations and the Use of Divine Names as Weapons." *Journal of Near Eastern Studies* 70: 207–27.

Lipinski, Edward. 1972. "The Goddess Aṯirat in Ancient Arabia, in Babylon, and in Ugarit." In *Orientalia Lovaniensia. Periodica 3,* 101–19. Louvain, Belgium: Instituut voor Oriëntalistiek.

Lucian. 1913. *The Syrian Goddess.* Translated by by Herbert A. Strong and John Garstang. London: Constable.

Magli, G. 2016. "Sirius and the Project of the Megalithic Enclosures at Gobekli Tepe." *Nexus Network Journal* 18: 337–46.

Malville, J. M., F. Wendorf, A. A. Mazar, and R. Schild. 1998. "Megaliths and Neolithic Astronomy in Southern Egypt." *Nature* 392: 488–90.

Malville, J. M., R. Schild, F. Wendorf, and R. Brenmer. 2007. "Astronomy of Nabta Playa." *African Skies/Cieux Africains* 11: 20–27.

Manning, W. 2015. "The Double Tradition of Aphrodite's Birth and Her Semitic Origins." *Scripta Mediterranea* 23.

Marinatos, Nanno. 2000. *Goddess and the Warrior: The Naked Goddess and Mistress of the Animals in Early Greek Religion.* London: Routledge.

McBeath, A., and A. D. Gheorghe. 2005. "Meteor Beliefs Project: Meteorite Worship in the Ancient Greek and Roman Worlds." *WGN, Journal of the International Meteor Organization* 33 (5): 135–44.

Merisante, Margaret. 2015. *Aloft into the Shining Skies: The Mythic Intersections of Celestial Mare Goddesses and Swan Maidens.* Paper presented at the 2015 Annual Meeting of the Pacific Northwest Region of the American Academy of Religion, Society of Biblical Literature. The American Schools of Oriental Research.

Metcalf, Christopher. 2019. "14. A Hymn to Nanaya." In *Sumerian Literary Texts in the Schøyen Collection: Volume 1: Literary Sources on Old Babylonian Religion,* 70–71. University Park: Penn State University Press.

Miller, Jared L. 2008. "Setting Up the Goddess of the Night Separately." In *Anatolian Interfaces: Hittites, Greeks and Their Neighbours*, edited by Billie Jean Collins, Mary R. Bachvarova, and Ian C. Rutherford, 67–72. Barnsley, UK: Oxbow Books.

Mondon, Geneviève. 2009. "D'Astarté à Tanit: Flaubert lecteur of *La Déessse Syrienne* de Samosate." *Études de genèse.*

Mouton, Alice. 2004. "Le rituel de Walkui (KBo 32.176): Quelques réflexions sur la déesse de la nuit et l'image du porc dans le monde hittite." *Zeitschrift für Assyriologie un Vorderasiatische Archäologie* 94: 85–105.

———. 2008. "Les divinités Mésopotamiennes de la nuit et la déesse de la nuit Hittite: Un cas d'emprunt?" In *Ktèma: Civilisations de l'Orient, de la Grèce et de Rome antiques*, N°33, 215–33.

Nilsson, Martin P. 1950. *Minoan-Mycenaen Religion, and Its Survival in Greek Religion.* New York: Biblo & Tannen.

Ornan, Tallay, 2004. "The Goddess Gula and Her Dog," *Israel Museum Studies in Archaeology* 3.

Papachatzis, Nicolaos. 1989. "The Cult of Erechtheus and Athena on the Acropolis of Athens." *Kernos* 2: 175–85.

Papamichali, Olga, Konstantinos Kalachanis, and Milan S. Dimitrjević. 2022. "The Bear Mythology: An Enduring Archetypical Tale of Feminine Empowerment, Adulthood and Motherhood. *Graeco-Latina Brunensia* 27 (2): 101–11.

Pausanias. 1918. *Description of Greece.* Vol. 1, books 1–2. Translated by W. H. S. Jones. Cambridge, MA: Harvard University Press.

Perdibon, A. 2019. *Mountains and Trees, Rivers and Springs. Animistic Beliefs and Practices in Ancient Mesopotamian Religion.* Wiesbaden, Germany: Harrassowitz Verlag.

PGM. 1992. *The Greek Magical Papyri in Translation, Including the Demotic Spells.* Edited by Hans Dieter Betz. Chicago: University of Chicago Press.

Pilipović, Sanja. 2001. "Divine Rape as Funeral Motif: Example of Stela from Viminacium." *Balcanica*, no. XXXII–XXXI: 61–89.

Pingree, David. 1989. "Indian Planetary Images and the Tradition of Astral Magic." *Journal of the Warburg and Courtauld Institutes* 52: 1–13.

Pliny. 1963. *Natural History, Volume VIII: Books 28–32.* Translated by W. H. S. Jones. Loeb Classical Library 418. Cambridge, MA: Harvard University Press.

Reiner, Erica. 1995. *Astral Magic in Babylonia.* Transactions of the American Philosophical Society, vol. 85, part 4. Philadelphia: American Philosophical Society.

Rhodius, Apollonius. 2016. *Argonautica.* Books 1–4. Translated by R. C. Seaton. London: Wentworth Press. First published 1912.

Roets, Merida. 2020. "Goats in the Ancient Near East and Their Relationship with the Mythology, Fairytale and Folklore of These Cultures," in *Goats (Capra)—From Ancient to Modern,* edited by Sándor Kukovics. London: IntechOpen.

Rogers, J. H. 1998. "Origins of the Ancient Constellations: I. The Mesopotamian Traditions." *Journal of the British Astronomical Association* 108: 9–28.

Sánchez-Quinto, F., H. Malmström, M. Fraser, L. Girdland-Flink, E. M. Svensson, L. G. Simões, R. George et al. 2019. "Megalithic Tombs in Western and Northern Neolithic Europe Were Linked to a Kindred Society." *Proceedings of the National Academy of Sciences of the United States of America* 116 (19): 9469–74.

Schmidt, Brian B. 1996. *Israel's Beneficent Dead: Ancestor Cult and Necromancy in Ancient Israelite Religion and Tradition.* Ann Arbor, MI: Eisenbrauns.

Schmitt, Rüdiger. 2013. "Astarte, Mistress of Horses, Lady of the Chariot: The Warrior Aspect of Astarte." *Die Welt Des Orients* 43 (2): 213–25.

Schuhmacher, Thomas. 2013. "Some Reflections about an Alabaster Stele from Mari (Syria) and Its Possible Relations to the Western Mediterranean." *Cuadernos de Prehistoria y Arqueología* 39: 7–20.

Serwint, Nancy. 2002. "Aphrodite and Her Near Eastern Sisters: Spheres of Influence." In *Aphrodite: Women and Society in Ancient Cyprus,* edited by Diane Bolger and Nancy Serwint, 325–50. Boston: American Schools of Oriental Research.

Shibata, Daisuke, and Shigeo Yamada, ed. 2021. *Calendars and Festivals in Mesopotamia in the Third and Second Millennia BC.* Studia Chaburensia 9. Wiesbaden, Germany: Harrassowitz.

Singer, Itamar. 2002. *Hittite Prayers.* Atlanta, CA: Society of Biblical Literature.

Smith, Kate. 2007. *Guides, Guards, and Gifts to the Gods: Domesticated Dogs in the Art and Archaeology of Iron Age and Roman Britain.* Oxford, UK: British Archaeological Reports.

Smith, Mark S. 2001. *The Origins of Biblical Monotheism: Israel's Polytheistic Background and the Ugaritic Texts.* Oxford, UK: Oxford University Press.

———. 2014. *The Ugaritic Baal Cycle.* Leiden, Netherlands: Brill.

Stadelmann, Rainer. 1975. "Astartepapyrus." In, *Lexikon der Ägyptologie,* edited by Wolfgang Helck and Eberhard Otto, 509–11. Wiesbaden, Germany: Harrassowitz Verlag.

Stavrakopoulou, Francesca. 2017. "The Ancient Goddess, the Biblical Scholar, and the Religious Past: Re-Imaging Divine Women." In *The Bible and Feminism: Remapping the Field,* edited by Yvonne Sherwood. Oxford, UK: Oxford Academic.

Steele, Laura. 2007. "Women and Gender in Babylonia." Chapter 21 in *The Babylonian World,* edited by Gwendolyn Leick, 299–316. Oxfordshire, UK: Routledge.

Steinkeller, Piotr. 1994. "Nanshe and the Birds." Paper for the Jacobsen Symposium.

Stol, Martin. 1998. "Nanaja." *Reallexikon der Assyriologie* 9: 146–51.

Streck, Michael P., and Nathan Wasserman. 2012. "More Light on Nanâya." *Zeitschrift fur Assyriologie und Vorderasiatische Archaelog* 102: 183–201.

Stuckey, Johanna H. 2003. "Goddess Anat: Warrior Virgin of the Ancient Levant." *MatriFocus* 3-1.

———. 2004. "Inanna, Goddess of 'Infinite Variety.'" *MatriFocus* 4-1.

———. 2005. "Ancient Mother Goddesses and Fertility Cults." *Journal of the Motherhood Initiative for Research and Community Involvement* 7 (1): 38.

———. 2006. "'Going to the Dogs': Healing Goddesses of Mesopotamia." *MatriFocus* 5-2.

———. 2008. "Spirit Possession and the Goddess Ishtar in Ancient Mesopotamia." *MatriFocus* 8-1.

———. 2009a. "Atargatis, the 'Syrian goddess.'" *MatriFocus* 8-3.

———. 2009b. "Tanit of Carthage." *MatriFocus* 8-4.

Sugimoto, David T., ed. 2014. *Transformation of a Goddess: Ishtar-Astarte-Aphrodite.* Fribourg, Switzerland: Academic Press Fribourg.

Svoronos, Jean N. 1894. "Britomartis, la soi-disant Europe sur le platane de Gortyne." *Revue belge de numismatique* 50: 113–47.

Tacitus. 1942. *Complete Works of Tacitus.* Edited by Moses Hadas. Translated by Alfred John Church and William Jackson Brodribb. New York: Random House. First published 1873.

Taylor, Lindsay. 2019. "The Snake Goddess Dethroned: Deconstructing the Work and Legacy of Sir Arthur Evans." Honors thesis, University of Maine.

Tully, Caroline, and Sam Crooks. 2015. "Dropping Ecstasy? Minoan Cult and the Tropes of Shamanism." *Time and Mind* 8 (2): 1–30.

Vasconcelos, J. Leite de. 1897. *Religiões da Lusitania na parte que principalmente se refere a Portugal*, vol. 1. Lisbon, Portugal: Imprensa Nacional.

Vianu, Maria Alexandrescu. 1997. "Aphrodites orientales dans le bassin du Pont-Euxin." *Bulletin de correspondance hellénique* 121: 15–32.

Walker, C. B. F., and Michael Dick. 2001. *The Induction of the Cult Image in Ancient Mesopotamia: The Mesopotamiam Mis Pi Ritual.* Helsinki: Neo-Assyrian Text Corpus Project, Institute for Asian and African Studies.

Watkins, Justin. 2007. "Athirat: As Found at Ras Shamra." *Studia Antiqua* 5, no. 1.

Wee, John Z. 2014. "Lugalbanda Under the Night Sky: Scenes of Celestial Healing in Ancient Mesopotamia." *Journal of Near Eastern Studies* 73, no. 1: 23–42.

West, David Reid. 1990. "Some Cults of Greek Goddesses and Female Daemons of Oriental Origin: Especially in Relation to the Mythology of Goddesses and Demons in the Semitic World." Ph.D. thesis, University of Glasgow.

White, Gavin. 2014. *Babylonian Star-Lore, an Illustrated Guide to the Star-Lore and Constellations of Ancient Babylonia.* London: Solaria Publications.

Wiggerman. F. A. M. 2011. "The Mesopotamian Pandemonium: A Provisional Census." *Studi e materiali di storia delle religioni* 77 (2): 298–322.

———. 1992. *Mesopotamian Protective Spirits.* Gronigen, Netherlands: Styx.

Wikander, Ola. 2014. *Drought, Death, and the Sun in Ugarit and Ancient Israel: A Philological and Comparative Study.* Coniectanea Biblica, Old Testament Series 61. Winona Lake, IN: Eisenbrauns.

Yılmaz, Derya. 2016. "Some Thoughts on the Troy Type Owl-Headed Idols of Western Anatolia." *Praehistorische Zeitschrift.*

Younger, K. Lawson. 2012. "Another Look at an Aramaic Astral Bowl." *Journal of Near Eastern Studies* 71 (2): 209–30.

Zangger, E., and R. Gautschy. 2019. "Celestial Aspects of Hittite Religion: An Investigation of the Rock Sanctuary Yazilikaya." *Journal of Skyscape Archaeology*, 5 (1): 5–38.

INDEX

BOOKS OF RELATED INTEREST

Womb Awakening
Initiatory Wisdom from the Creatrix of All Life
by Seren Bertrand and Azra Bertrand, M.D.

Magdalene Mysteries
The Left-Hand Path of the Feminine Christ
by Seren Bertrand and Azra Bertrand, M.D.

Return of the Divine Sophia
Healing the Earth through the Lost Wisdom
Teachings of Jesus, Isis, and Mary Magdalene
by Tricia McCannon

The Gospel of Mary Magdalene
by Jean-Yves Leloup
Foreword by Jacob Needleman

The Way of the Wild Soul Woman
5 Earth Archetypes to Unleash Your Full Feminine Power
by Mary Reynolds Thompson
Foreword by Clare Dubois

Witch Wisdom for Magical Aging
Finding Your Power through the Changing Seasons
by Cait Johnson
Foreword by Caitlín Matthews

Sage, Huntress, Lover, Queen
Access Your Power and Creativity through Sacred Female Archetypes
by Mara Branscombe

INNER TRADITIONS • BEAR & COMPANY
P.O. Box 388
Rochester, VT 05767
1-800-246-8648
www.InnerTraditions.com

Or contact your local bookseller